THE UNITED STATES OF AMERICA
FEDERAL RESERVE NOTE
THIS NOTE IS LEGAL TENDER FOR ALL DEBTS, PUBLIC AND PRIVATE
WASHINGTON, D.C.
G 05555555 A
ONE HUNDRED DOLLARS
100

Millionaire Status

21st Century Millionaires Showcased Inside

Dr. Israel Prince

Kingdom Dominion One

Unless otherwise indicated, all scriptural quotations are from the King James Version of the Bible.

Published by Kingdom Dominion Enterprises

Millionaire Status Psychological Programming System
Dr. Israel Prince Barsh, B.A. D. Div.
Published by: Kingdom Dominion Publishers

Printed in the United States of America

Dedication

Millionaire Status Psychological Program System *is dedicated To my Seven sons, Millionaire's (MIT's) Prince's, Joshuael, R-jay, Isaiah, Caleb, Joseph, Isaac, and Josiah, whom I love dearly, this system is dedicated to you, to your children's children that as I have deposited in you, rehearse in their ears and deposit in their spirit for Generations of Millionaire's Protégé's.. May you magnetize the Grandeur of life, as JOB 22:24* **"Thou and thy children shall lay up GOLD AS DUST, excel to serve the world and be a Millionaire by 30 years old!"**

Imagination is more important than knowledge, your thoughts are your coming attraction . . . . *Albert Einstein*

It takes a deaf man to hear . . . . *Thomas Edison*

Art is not truth; art is a lie that makes us realize truth . . . . *Pablo Picasso*

Lead, follow, or get out of the way . . . . *Ted Turner*

Don't listen to the market researchers . . . . *Steven Jobs (Apple Computer)*

A computer on every desk in every home . . . . *Bill Gates*

You have to believe in the Impossible . . . . *Howard Hughes*

Personal Power comes from Mental independence . . . All Great men were independent Thinkers. . . . . *Theron Dumont*

Edison, Picasso, Einstein were creative geniuses who learned early that it was not necessary to "buy into," the corporate womb in order to achieve success, they challenge the Status Quo . . . . *Gene Landrum*

Special Salute

To Countless Mentors who shoulders I stand on, to Prophet James Giles, extraordinary author, I appreciate your hours of depositing wisdom, laughing and being a true friend.

To Beverly Symes, of "Symes Graphic Design", awesome book lay out, image cover design of complete book, thanks for the hours of counsel in finishing this book, I recommend colleagues to utilize your gift!

To Queen Gerri, my soul mate, who has continued to go the distance in pursuit of Truth. Your angelic patience and loving energy, editing late at night enabled this project to be completed and our lives to be forever changed.

What Top Endorsers Are Saying About *Millionaire Status*

If you are ready for an ELECTRIFYING, SHACKLE-BREAKING, 'INNER-GIZING,' MINDSET-SHIFTING, POSSIBILITY-CREATING book, then you are ready for MILLIONAIRE STATUS!! Once you read this book, you will not perceive yourself, your divine assignment, God, money, your relationship to money, or wealth the same, ever again!!

Dr. Israel Barsh has profound insight, wisdom, and soul-stirring truth and power in the pages of his book.

I read every word of it in a single sitting! I couldn't put it down. It had me riveted!

Amen!! Hallelujah! This book sets you FREE!!!!

Debrena Jackson Gandy, Best-selling author (Sacred Pampering Principles, All the Joy You Can Stand), Transformational Speaker, National Seminar Leader, Entrepreneur, Joy and Ease Coach

Dr. Israel Prince has written a third millennium primer for those seeking another level of Kingdom wisdom and manifestation. Broadly researched, it combines spiritual and practical principles - keys to creating a wealth consciousness that produces tangible results. This book could launch a much needed revolution in the earth. God delights in the prosperity of those whom He has created in His own image and likeness. It is the original intent of God that man live in the garden of delights; that he enjoy wholeness, health, wisdom, wealth, joy, creativity, productivity, and bliss in this dimension of living.

For those of you that will read, meditate, and apply the principles in this provocative treatise. Teach others to do the same, you will be well on your way to fulfilling the Divine Plan for your own life and for that of humanity.

James L Giles, Prophet
Author, International Speaker
Charlotte, North Carolina

"In his book Millionaire Status, Dr. Barsh not only reveals to us the principles of success. He introduces us to the laws of possibilities. This book will not only inspire you, it will challenge you to think and move forward."

Tony Morris
New Covenant Christian Center, Seattle, WA

You now have the tool to manifest all your dreams into reality. When you pick up this book, you are picking up the *heartbeat* of God for the great transfer of wealth (Proverbs 1 3:22). By familiarizing us with people who have reached "Millionaire Status," Dr. Barsh builds the faith of a reader to prosper with Kingdom concepts and purpose.

Kevin J. Gerald
Covenant Celebration Champion Center
Tacoma, Washington

Dr. Israel's insight and revelation, which he so graciously and articulately shares in *Millionaire Status*, is like a beacon at sea. My prayer is that everyone who is floundering in "poverty thinking" and financial confusion would see that light and gravitate toward it—it will change their lives.

Jim Folger
Regional Director, InventHelp
Seattle, WA

There is no lack in the kingdom of God, Our Heavenly Father desires that we "prosper and be in health, even as our soul prospers" (3 John 1:2). **Millionaire Status** is **Powerful - Dynamic - Informative and Instructional.** This book will inspire you to step up and begin to believe God for you financial success!!!!!! It will stir your faith and enlighten you on what the Supreme banker and Holder of Wealth has to say about finances. I encourage you to read it, meditate on it, apply it, and let the blessings begin.

Bishop Lenall Battle
Unity Christian Ministries (FODC)
Fellowship of Deliverance Churches Inc.

When you read this book you will discover God's principles of economics that will unleash wealth in your life. Prophet Barsh through divine revelation of God's Word will take you the reader to another level of spiritual understanding of money. If you put into practice these Kingdom principles you will experience a supernatural flow of wealth in your life. This book is a much-needed reading for the body of Christ.

Ken Rose Sr.
New Life Embassy

Millionaire Status Vision

To ignite a Generation of brilliant minds, entrepreneurs, business strategists and millionaire's who together will train every young mind in the Universe to believe and imagine impossibilities as possibilities.

Contents

Dedication v

Millionaire Status Vision x

Introduction xii

Make The Paradigm Power Shift 9

Psychological Programming System 11

Releasing the Millionaire's Genius E-zine 51

Money Magnetism 75

Millionaire's Mindset in the Making 79

Millionaire's Shift in Consciousness 109

Millionaire Shift to Kingdom 123

Millionaire Kings Movement! 131

Millionaire Power Shifting In the New Millennium 137

Millionaire Activation 145

Manifesting Millionaire Mindset
Through Daily Wealth Meditations 159

Introduction

You are not reading *Millionaire Status* by coincidence or accident. The sovereign ability of the Father of the universe has drawn you to this dynamic book to cause you to express yourself at the highest level. **Your purchasing of this book is a declaration that you are ready to make the Paradigm shift to unleash your greatness to the earth!** You are tired of being apart of the, "Status Quo", the call of greatness is within. Now that you have separated yourself from the crowd, you are about to experience Quantum leaps in increasing your personal power in attracting wealth.

This book was sent by God to challenge you to make a power shift in your consciousness and cause you to manifest riches that will affect you down to your fourth generation.

God the Chief Executive Officer (C.E.O) of the universe, administrator of blessings and creator of the world, created you with himself in mind. You are his original design, predecessor of all that belong to him, his number one interest in the earth. You are here by divine ordination, not here by accident or coincident, but by the sovereign will of the creator of the universe.

Millionaire Status is designed to liberate people from the system of poverty and to magnetize wealth in all realms of their lives. The Mandate is to teach every *face on the planet that there is a MILLIONAIRE IN EVERY ONE and the only class you belong in is called Dominion. In Greek, Dominion means having the ability to determine your own destiny regardless of race, creed or color..*

I was raised in **a religious system.** As my spirit was growing, I would ask ministers "How come we are not rich?" "Why are there no millionaires in the church?" "Why are people not happy, fulfilled and sad all the time until Sunday morning?" Their response was always the same "Trust the Lord." "Wait on God." My favorite "You will be blessed after while." After a while the only thing that came was debt, bills and more unfulfillment. People in my HOOD were religious junkie's who got high on Sunday lived in the dungeon on Monday, while other nations were producing, they remained consumers.

Millionaires Think Outside Of A System

I learned that these responses were due to a lack of knowledge and themselves not actually knowing the answer. Through my continuous growth, development and vigorous study of God's word, I came to understand that the minister's didn't have an answer that they were programmed by a system that keeps them in poverty. As a result, I felt so strongly led to do whatever I can to help people learn how to eradicate poverty from their lives. Millionaire

Status was birthed as a thirst for wisdom and to help search for the truth to answer my questions.

Catherine Ponder states, "Poverty is a form of hell caused by man's blindness to God's unlimited good for him." It's a form of disease and insanity.

I was raised in the land of the beautiful with a great American **educational system**, yet I graduated with peers who couldn't read their own diplomas. Five years later 35% of my graduating class had fallen through the cracks, on drugs and/or still looking for a job. Why weren't they taught how to become an entrepreneur? Why weren't they taught how to become a millionaire by the age of 30? There are over 400 million people in the US, yet 95 % of them live the majority of their lives in a poverty state. I am determined to reach the 95% with this system to deprogram the poverty mind, wake their consciousness from the sedative thought of instant gratification and get rich quick schemes, to undue the Hypnotic spells of commercialize credit cards traps and **release the millionaire in every man.**

Activate & Accelerate Your First Million Dollar!

Get ready to be orbited in profound wisdom revelation and to shape your ultimate reality. For the next 60 days , I suggest you don't put this system down, take notes, create a rich habit of magnetically drawing clients, contracts, people, new money, new travel, business expansion, new health, relationships and wealth in your life. If you are married, buy your spouse a system. If you are a business owner, pastor, or business leader, invest in the personal growth of your entire corporation, and increase their MONEY MAGNETISM! Now place demands on yourself to express and release "the Magic in you" at the highest level.

Dr. Israel Prince

THE UNITED STATES OF AMERICA
FEDERAL RESERVE NOTE
ONE HUNDRED DOLLARS
THIS NOTE IS LEGAL TENDER FOR ALL DEBTS, PUBLIC AND PRIVATE
WASHINGTON, D.C.
G 05555555 A
100

Consciousness Is Everything

The first principle of coming into prosperity **is breaking out of a system that breeds a consciousness of poverty.** I continued to study, develop and clean out my "hard drive." Soon, my hard drive (consciousness) was cleaned and I had a new programming system. A Wealth system that brought prosperity, fulfillment and universal abundance.

Programming begins in early childhood development where your parents are your teachers. You have been taught to do as other's do and live like the majority of the people live, working a job or in a career that is unfulfilled and unrewarding. The probability is that you are not satisfied with your present condition. You are tired of living from paycheck to paycheck. You are tired of being a broke Christian. You have tithed, gave offerings and still have not seen the manifestation of your dreams. You have been asking for your breakthrough. Your desire is to be a millionaire. ***Now you have in hand the, "Millionaire System"!*** You thirst for the finest, the most elegant and the finer things in life; you have astronautic taste, endowed with the image of greatness. But you don't know why it has not manifested.

For long enough you have allowed situations, circumstances, mistakes, mind sets opinions of others men and relationships to handicap God's purpose for your life. Divine opportunity has knocked again. Get ready to be restored to God's Original Design for your life. Whenever God wanted something, infinite wisdom created it. There are million dollar ideas inside of you that lay dormant, but are ready to be unleashed by your genius powers.

Growth Demands Change!

There is a Million Dollar ideal inside of you to change the consciousness and complex of Nations! The storm, the crisis was sent to catapult you to the next level. Dry your tears, stop weeping about what happened, it was ordained before the foundation of the world and now you must MOVE! Eagles fly in the air. No more waiting on the crowd's opinion about God's destiny for your life, this is your season for divine overflow blessings! The latter shall be greater than the former!

MILLIONAIRE AGENDA

Millionaire Status is, first, designed to unveil to you the supernatural purpose of your being in the earth, and then to acquaint you with wealth to fulfill the countless dreams and visions of the father. You were genetically engineered and originally made to be co-creator, co-manager in the exact design of the maker of the universe to demonstrate kingdom riches in all realms of life. This book will teach you how to release the millions of possibilities within you.

Millionaire Status is for 21st Century forerunners, dreamers, pioneers, trailblazers, entrepreneurs who are called to birth new paths and new realities. Get ready to . . .

- dismantle negative sabotaging beliefs and ideas
- release past experiences, relationships
- detoxify negative energy that has blocked the abundance flow
- Cultivate a Millionaire mindset
- Dethrone religious myths about money.

Millionaire Status Will:

- Identify the systems of economics, society norms, philosophies, ideologies, and religious beliefs of man that have handicapped, sabotaged and paralyzed human potential and businesses.
- Create a consciousness to increase your personal magnetism to attract wealth.
- Identify and eradicate limiting beliefs, negative images, creeds and philosophies from one's mentality.
- Unveil to you to enter the Higher Dimensions of fulfilling the divine purpose of your higher self in the Earth! Forces of Angels have hidden the codes to your gift to serve the world and humanity by releasing your highest contribution. The Bible says people are destroyed because of the lack of knowledge.
- Harness and awake the powers to open up the, creative imagination for employees, business leaders, corporations, church leaders, colleges, institutions, schools and emerging entrepreneurs who want to maximize and create a synergy to receive the transfer of wealth.

Psychological Programming System

The Psychological Programming System (PPS) is designed to create Millionaires and teach individuals to understand the Divine principles of the universe, activate business owners, individuals, entrepreneurs and youth to release their Millionaire Genius-ezine (unfathomable abilities) that have been sabotaged by systems. To open up the creative mind to manifest money, wealth, and be a millionaire!

When you install this system in the mind (consciousness), you will create a *positive blueprint* to attract wealth, prosperity & abundance. The process of laying a foundation of rich ideas, rich feelings, and abundance in mentality reflects as *Jesus spoke, "A good man will bring forth good things out of the foundation of his heart."*

IT'S YOUR SEASON! For too long the world has celebrated the accomplishments of people of the past who are dead. COME ALIVE! There is a fresh dream in you. Come into your Einstein moment.

Millionaire Status Principle #1

Recognize Your Genetic Makeup

Millionaire DECREE!

Stop right here, right now and decree: I am ready to go to the Next Level! I am coming out of my grave clothes of yesterday. I am loosing myself from the tomb of the past; past debts, past pains, past relationships. I am unlocking my destiny!

You are a MILLIONAIRE IN THE MAKING. When God created you, God had himself in mind and no matter where you are in life; God is not through making you into a double diamond. Million dollar ideas have been locked inside of you and not released. That's why you purchased this system. You're behind time. Countless inventions, awards, feats, discoveries have been waiting on you to find this system. It's time you get in step with God's time table for your life! No more dreams turning to nightmares. No more visions turning to fantasies. This is your prophetic moment!

No matter who has given up on you, God is not through with you yet. Silver is being turned to gold. As you program your self for success, for wealth, for prosperity, you will manifest exact images, exact pictures, and exact feelings by application of the ***Psychological Programming System.***

Robert T. Kiyosaki stated in his book, Rich Dad, Poor Dad, "The poor and the middle class work for money, the rich make money."

Thoughts are MOVING FORCES. THOUGHTS OF WEALTH ATTRACT WEALTH. To eradicate poverty from your existence is not just knowing the King, but applying the Kings principles as a system of life! Rich people don't worry about money, they create it from within! Creator's create, creatures exist. Creator's produce, while poor people consume. Poor people work for money, rich make money to work for them. Rich create capital, poor people create debt. A poverty mind will produce more poverty. Surround yourself with rich dresses, rich interior and rich people.
Think and grow rich!

The mind is a terrible thing to waste. ***Now you must answer your univer-***

sal call of magnetizing, attracting, vibrating and creating wealth, release the drum major instinct inside of you and lead the world band!

Millionaire Status Principle #2

The Mind of the Maker is the Mind of Man

The most single asset you have is your **MIND**! Ninety-nine percent of people allow other's to mine their mind 24 hours a day, 365 days a year. They sell their mind to the highest bidder instead of learning the art of manifesting from within! You have to grasp the concept that money is not real. Money is a consciousness. It is a symbol. Consciousness is the only currency.

If the mind is trained well, if it is conditioned perfectly, wealth can be created, unfathomed, unrealized and even far beyond the riches of King Solomon in the Bible. The masses are controlled by the systems of the world. You are not waiting on God. God is divine wisdom and has placed a million dollar idea inside of you that is lying dormant! **AWAKE THE MILLIONAIRE!**

Psalms 8:4-6 Man the Universe Apex of creation,

The Manifestation Creative Process (MCP) resides in the corridors of man's unlimited consciousness that was engineered with:

- Infinite supreme intelligence
- Light and illumination by the father of the Universe
- A nucleus that manufacturers all matters
- The divine make up

You are a created being who is made up of the same creative substance as God. A molecular structure that consists of atoms, electron and protons that created the universe, over 400 billion galaxies and named all the stars. All this POWER resides in you! May the divine powers of the universe shine upon you, enlighten your consciousness, elevate your thoughts, and magnetize the exact purposes of your creation.

"For thou hast made him a little lower than the angels, and hast crowned him with glory and honor, made him to have dominion over all the works of thy hands, place all things under his feet."

Now you have the operating manual and software to be installed in you, the God system, consciousness that has no limitations, no boundaries, no enemies and invincible abilities. A mind with depths of thousands of oceans, infinite potentials, inside of you in the ROCK OF AGES!

Learn how to deprogram & dismantle ***the negative, sabotaging Psychological Belief System (PBS), i***deas, past experiences, mind sets and religious myths about money, relationships and wealth.

Empower your self three-fold with this Millionaire Status System!

Know the power of being a money/people magnet! Right thoughts equal right results! Positive thoughts equal positive outcomes!

The Mind of the Maker is the Mind of Man

Millionaire Status Principle #3

INSTALL A NEW

Economic! Spiritual! Relational

Blueprint System

Why is it that you put money in your account but ***you still have holes in your pocket?*** Why does it seem that you have been to every conference in the world yet still not walking in Wealth?

Why does it seem that you have been in one relationship after another only to find that you are still unhappy and still unsatisfied?? Now you are taking on old cycle of your past, Tuesdays you feel suicidal and after 20 years the church is still killing chickens to raise money for the building fund and programs (ministries) that don't exist.

The prognosis is a negative program that is being transported through generations and will continue to mutate as a virus to the next generation until it has been destroyed. There is a negative blueprint in all three areas, **economic, spiritual** and **relational**, that has to be deleted off your mental system. Change the channel, then you will change what's appearing on your screen of life. Tired of low finances, reprogram wealth. Tired of wrong relationships, delete the negative ideas of men and women.

Transform your Money Blueprint to a positive to manifest riches. Change your relational blueprint to magnetize right relationships and change your spiritual blueprint to understand that you can have riches here and now (understanding a spiritual mind is not a religious mind). Fire the thieves in your mind to prevent them form stealing the destiny God has designed for you!

Caution! Now you have the fuel for excellence, to get the results from this system. You have to immediately start daily deleting, downloading, and cleansing your old negative PPS from your consciousness. Start RIGHT HERE, RIGHT NOW installing activate *positive* thoughts about money, wealth, relationships to manifest at your highest level. Before you install, cleanse and **Detox your mind from any negative thought, image, vibrations and words about money.** Keep a daily journal of your progress. Sow the Millionaires dream seeds into your mind at least three times daily to excel your growth.

Stop waiting on the crowd for permission. God already ordained it! Today become the P.U.S.H. (Prophesy Until Something Happen) of your predestine dreams. Prophesy over your self, push until something happen!

Millionaire Status Principle #4

You are an EVENT on the way to happen

You have realized you are not a part of the Status Quo mentality. Your purchasing this system is a prophetic declaration that you are ready to shift, while others are getting ready to pack their dreams away to the future. You are a modern day genius who cannot be held in the bondage of poverty. Get ready to unleash your gifts to the world! You are an event on the way to happen!

There is a million dollar idea inside of you to change the consciousness and complex of nations. The storm (crisis) was sent to catapult you to the next level. It was ordained before the foundation of the world, now you must **move**.

Millionaire Status System is not for the lazy mind. The mind that is stuck on **off**. This is not a get-rich quick scheme. This is a **SYSTEM**! You cannot place a large dream in a small mind. The Millionaire Status System will work for anyone at any age, race, and situation.

KINGDOMPRENEURS!

This system is designed to create what we call **Kingdompreneurs.** They have the GIFT OF MONEY but their skill has not been recognized by their leadership. Many **Kingdompreneurs** are locked in religious systems singing in choirs and are in poverty because they are in the wrong lane. This Millionaire System is focused on creating wealth protégé's of Queen Sheba's and King Solomon's and usher in dynasties of individual who will manifest wealth products, inventions, discoveries to market to Nations, retail stores, & corporations.

"And be not conformed to this world (systems) be ye transformed by the renewing of your mind, meaning "Unleash your entrepreneurs abilities, replace your 9-5 salary and create your own business, Stop allowing the unbelief of others handicap your dream and paralyze your ambitions.

Millionaire Status Principle #5

CASH FLOW + CAPITAL = Millionaire Status if you start with a definite plan with definite purpose. Set the course and stay on it!

Be determined to break out of the systematic lifestyle of working an 8-5 job. Ninety five percent of Millionaire's were not born with a silver spoon in their mouth, they activated a CASH FLOW SYSTEM to develop the CAPITAL to invest in stock, mutual funds, bonds, property and investment options at an early age to retire at age 31.

Everything in life operates on a system. You can't walk, talk or eat without your central nervous, involuntary and voluntary, and circulatory systems

working as God designed them! Your body is a self-healing and self-restoring system! You need a MONEY SYSTEM TO BE RICH!

Money Detoxification Ritual

Daily be detoxed from poison negative programming, negative words, images, beliefs, vibrations , arguments which have blocked your Money MAGNETISM detoxed from ideas, thoughts, religious misnomers about money being evil, money is good, money is currency, money is pure energy of love. Detox your business; detox your mind from thoughts which have not vibrated to attract wealth. You must at this point become a money magnet, allow money to circulate, allow money to breathe, you deserve to have money! Begin today to say I AM MONEY. MONEY COMETH! Money chases ideals; money chases my multi-million dollar ideas.

Thou shall Mediate day and night, observe to do all, you shall make thy way prosper and have good success in all the affairs of life. (Josh 1:8)

Millionaire Status Principle #6

Have a Break –out!

Break out of systematic thinking, break out of the traditional religious imprisonment, bondage of poverty and all genius's

Thought outside of the status quo! You are a trailblazer, you are a pathfinder, you are not called to follow old paths, and it's a new day! Renew you mind. Get in step with all the father has decreed in your name! Loose thyself from the dust and residue of yesterday!

You can't use the internet without a system server. You can't fix your car stereo without a system manual and you can't get rich without a MILLIONAIRE SYSTEM!

Millionaire Status System will only work when installed in emerging hungry tigers and eagles of the New Millennium who are ready to make a Paradigm Shift from the old to the new.

Albert Einstein was the acknowledged scientific genius of the nuclear age; Pablo Picasso was the most revered and idolized painter of the twentieth century and Thomas Edison was the most prolific inventor in history. They defied the odds, raised the standard of excellence beyond the imagination of mere men and super beings of there day.

Now, you know God has spoken a dynamic creative word inside of you. The Millionaire Genius has awakened inside of you and you are ready to advance.

MAKE THE PARADIGM POWER SHIFT

Now you have the system in hand to assist you in making the paradigm shift in your life.

Making a POWER SHIFT is imperative as 3rd millennium citizens. As business leaders, pastors, corporate presidents and family's one cannot do what the past generation did. Break the traditional norms of maintenance living to create capital to empower nations with an economic agenda.

The word **power** denotes ability, strength. **Shift** means to change courses. **Power shift is imperative** because one cannot use the models of the 60s with the present generation mind sets. Times have changed to lifestyles of a fast society. Millionaire opportunities have progressed with new and advanced software technology systems that include the internet superhighway. This has opened up the gateway for E-commerce businesses. Telecommunications are no longer monopolized. This has not only opened the channel for more innovative ways to communicate but has allowed people to create competition in the cellular business.

Some of the most catastrophic world events have also opened the door to creating millionaires. The Y2K put people and companies in a panic which others took advantage of by writing books and facilitating preparedness seminars for corporations. Moreover, 911 opened opportunities for people who were a part of this terrorism attack. Some of the people took photographs and sold them, while others wrote books and published documents on the tragic event. Now, there is a movie. In spite of any tragic world event, millionaires continue to be produced because they made a consciousness shift.

There has to be a shift in consciousness in the way you do business.

Millionaires are RISK TAKERS!

Now you have the system to assist you in making the Paradigm Shift! Whenever God wanted something, infinite wisdom created it. Millions of possibilities are ready to be unleashed by your genius powers!

Bill Gates will go down in history as the youngest self-made billionaire ever. His early 1992 stock jumps have placed his net worth at an estimated $7.4 billion. How did he do it? Gates created MS-DOS the industry-standard PC operating system for IBM where 90% of the world's computers use his system, and at the stroke of genius reserved the rights to sell it to any competitor of IBM.

Bill Gates tapped into his Millionaire-Billionaire Genius-ezine. My assignment is to teach, reach by radio and TV and get this book in the hands of 6.6 billion people on this planet. This book will teach people how to release their creative mind and their Millionaire–ezine!

You have astronomical powers, abilities and genetic genes to create the same substance that was created by the universe residing inside of you. At will it will manifest wealth, health, prosperity and happiness!

Infinite wisdom has created a system inside of you, when programmed, it can manifest anything. Install this creative system and start today! To captivate and move to your highest self, meditate, take notes daily and keep a journal on your progress.

You have the same divine creative spirit DIVINE SPARK AS JESUS CHRIST, that was in all great men like, Shakespeare, Napoleon, Picasso, Emerson, Einstein, Socrates and Aristotle. The only difference is they maximized their MIND POWER. You can develop this Personal Magnetism and rise above your fellows, above your present superiors, get out of POVERTY demeaning environments, train your mental forces to Magnetize desires thru the power of deliberate CONCENTRATION. Step into your POWER!

"MAXIMIZE PRODUCTIVITY IN INDIVIDUAL LEADERS, BUSINESS, CORPORATIONS, CHURCHES INCREASE OPTIMUM LEVEL OF PERFORMANCE!"

Millionaires in the Making Training is presently being inserted as pilot programs in schools, churches, corporations, Universities and colleges across this nation. This Psychological Programming System, first, identifies the scotomas or hidden blind spots in FRONTLINE LEADERS, managers and business teams challenging them to Magnetize & Attract Wealth.

MITM will activate consultants then establish a new paradigm of advance thinking software installed in their mind designed to open up their creative FLOW and allow the highest optimum level performance in all areas of life i.e. finances, business, organization goals and progressively increase clients and success.

Contact Dr. Israel at *kingdomdominion1@earthlink.net* to receive a free consultation today.

Manifest at the highest level Achieving Excellence in business.

THE UNITED STATES OF AMERICA
FEDERAL RESERVE NOTE
ONE HUNDRED DOLLARS
THIS NOTE IS LEGAL TENDER FOR ALL DEBTS, PUBLIC AND PRIVATE
G 05555555 A
WASHINGTON, D.C.
100

CHAPTER 1

Psychological Programming System

Stretch Into Divine Purpose

This process will stretch you into a Divine purpose to enjoy all that the Universe has deemed yours. This is not an exhaustive study but is a tremendous investigative tool, a complete *Psychological Programming System (PPS)* to make you **awareness** of your **Money Blueprint**, then **understand** how you receive it, then **execute** the right commands in consciousness to change it.

> ***Money Blueprint**: How your present reality forecasts whether you have been psychologically programmed with images, imprints, conditioning which repel wealth, or a limiting image which minimizes abundance, or a mindset which sabotages relationships, wealth, and health.*

Millionaire Status Principle #7

Recognize Now I am a Millionaire in the Making

Millionaire: *(Greek meaning)* **(1)** *Possessing abundance of material possessions, mentally sharp, physically fit, socially healthy, emotionally stable.* **(2)** *Financially secured above measure; able to invest without caution; having surplus to give to many; a person of great* *influence, affluence, wealth, wisdom, skill, and esteem; one who has a net-worth of over one hundred thousand dollars.*

Once you delete all the negative programming and install in your mind the **Positive Prosperity Program**, you will come into your divine flow of prosperity to manifest, to birth, and to make visible to the eye the ideal perfect reality.

Everything you can imagine will appear! You are a promise with infinite possibilities. The key inside is the new software to install for prosperity result immediately.

There are several Biblical words for prosperity: *Tsaleach,* meaning to push forward, to break out, to break mightily, and to be profitable; *Sakal*, meaning to be or act intelligent, to be skilled, expert, prudent, and to have good success. *Shalom*, meaning to be safe, well, happy, at peace, and whole; *Tselach,* meaning to advance, be beautiful, be favorable, and a place in consciousness called; *Jabe',* meaning to expand, to enlarge, and to stretch your territory to become a ruler.

This system goes beyond renewing the mind. It is a primary concept designed to:

- Take you back to God's original purpose for man to rule and create form his on paradise.
- To change your **negative conditioning** this will result in manifestations in your life from low finances to walking in wealth.
- To change the cycle of wrong relationships to ideal soul mate.
- To change the results of business failure (to save a dying business, you will need to overhaul your complete system from the roots and deleted off your old mental programming to allow the new software to work).

Imagination is more important than knowledge!

—Albert Einstein

What Is the Catalyst for Creative Behavior?

Is there an innate personality gene, an inborn trait of talent as is common believed? Is heredity more critical than environment? It would seem not, if you consider the histories of great millionaire geniuses Edison, Picasso, and Einstein. Freud hypothesized that our personalities become indelibly imprinted between the ages of five and eight. No doubt many of our behavioral idiosyncrasies and traits have **been formed due to imprinting, and conditioned by this early age.**

We conclude that conditioning, environmental imprints are the major cause to the creative force within a man.

Robert Kiyosaki, *in his book,* ***"Rich Dad, Poor Dad"*** *states "The problem I sense today is that there are millions of people who feel guilty about greed. It's an old conditioning form in their past childhood. Their desire to have the finer things, the luxury cars, the million dollar estates, have been denied due to their subconscious. ...* ***Access denied*** *due to a negative blueprint in their hard drive."*

Millionaire Status Principle #8

Become aware of your Money Blueprint and understand how your mind has been conditioned to think outside of your Millionaire Destiny!

Then recondition your subconscious by applying this system each day in forming new habits, thoughts, and beliefs. The result will magnetize your wealth, affluence and influence, and help you to form the right relationships that will increase your opportunities and take you to the next level. If you desire to be a part of the "rich and the famous," then act like it, think like it, dress like it, speak like it, and above all stop apologizing for your rights as the child of a king.

Then the major goal becomes **executing the commands in your consciousness** in changing out the old paradigms and implementing the new.

What is a Blueprint?

It is the precise vision of the finished product in your mind.

It's the exact image, the exact measurement of your success potential similar to the specific drawings to be given to an architect to design a house, building or facility. It's an intended guide to producing a finished product.

Your Money Blueprint

Understand your present money blueprint.

An architect cannot build a house without exact images, rooms and the specifications of walls printed on a *blueprint.* Each person has either a positive or negative blueprint imprinted inside of them from early childhood that has ***conditioned*** their thoughts to produce a certain reality. If you have a positive blueprint toward riches, then you will easily attract wealth. You will radiate and vibrate the right energy to magnetize it to you. If you have a negative blueprint, this will prevent you from manifesting God's ideal for your life. Your energy will have to vibrate at the level of desire.

How Do I?

- Manifest the right relationship
- Meet my ideal soul mate
- Own my own business
- Gain prosperity, weight loss, more self esteem, happiness, more friends, a fun life
- Increase members in my organization
- Break old cycles of my past
- Create the life I desire
- Stop living from paycheck to paycheck

The manifestation process starts inside of you.

Woman with the issue of blood for 12 long years said within her self.... if I can ......then I will be made ....

Millionaire Status Principle #9

You manifest by thinking, feeling, and imagining it is done.

This is why you must first cleanse your internal blueprints of all negative events, experiences, negative programs, words, and thoughts of your past.

Millionaire Status Principle #10

Manifest: ***(Greek) to birth forth, to materialize, and to bring forth from the divine substance within invisible to the visible. Manifestation process births new realities out of ones spirit, with the creative force of the tongue.***

The crash of 1929 was a psychological panic; it was fear seizing the minds of people everywhere. Most problems reside first on the psychic level and then move to the material level. *Fear* is false evidences appearing real. While CEO's on one side of the world were jumping out of windows, on the other side of the world, WALT DISNEY was making billions with a cartoon animation called Mickey Mouse. (Read more about Walt Disney in the chapter on Millionaire Profiles)

Become aware of what type of destiny you desire, understand how to get it, execute, take action and pursue it!

These following concepts represent the 3 stages of the proper mindset in manifesting the vision in your life, family, business and world community:

- Awareness
- Understanding
- Execution

Awareness, Understanding and Execution

People are constantly *broadcasting* their internal money blueprint, especially whenever they don't have a tangible substance of money. Their reactions reflect their money blueprint. Many become depressed, angry, frustrated and nervous shutting down until money manifests. This explains why couples who have different money blueprints and a different wealth consciousness it's difficult to manifest. Their energy is oppositional; their thought waves broadcast negative vibrations toward money so money is not attracted to them. If you only have peace when you get paid, then GOD is not your source, money is.

Money is to be the servant, not the boss.

A couple, business, church and mastermind group who cultivate their mind will have the same money blueprint, exact images of wealth and radiate prosperity energy will change nations. Ninety-nine percent people on the planet have a negative blueprint toward wealth, health, relationships and prosperity that has to be uninstalled. These people have to install a complete new psychological positive blueprint that will in one year attract more wealth, peace and a loving relationship. By simply changing the internal locus of control you interrupt the cycle that your grandmother, mother, father, brother(s) and sister(s) who have never produced wealth.

Millionaire Status Principle #11

The universe is user friendly for whatever you desire to attract. Use the Law of Attraction and you will attract more of what's already in you.

Many will never create wealth because of the poverty blueprint inside of their consciousness that cancels the creative flow. Many women and men want to get married, but the problem is they have never been single and they haven't released there past relationships, past hurts and past pain. They keep replaying the events of the past in new relationships!

This is why a person who wins the lottery in one year loses all their money; this is why many individuals can't keep relationships, jobs and always have money problems because they have an ingrained negative program which continues to break down their life. You simply must change the money software inside of you. Poverty, like prosperity, is a program!

Awareness

Where did you get your Money blueprint from? Your health blueprint determines whether you will be healthy or overweight. Everything in life has a foundation, a blueprint, images, imprints; conditioning derived from parents, uncles, aunties, friends, religious and education systems. "Change the imprints, change the results, you will manifest what you dwell on!

I was recently at my bank ATM machine and was so excited to use my new ATM card and access new money. I put the card in the machine and the words "ACCESS DENIED" appeared on the screen. I just knew I put in the right password. So I tried again. Again, "ACCESS DENIED." I called my wife and humbly asked for the password. Well, as you might have guessed, I had the wrong password and so the system rejected it.

The reason many haven't been able to manifest wealth, health, prosperity, new money, estates, and right relationships is because they continued to force the wrong code into a Universe that desires to give them prosperity. For over 20 years, they have received an "ACCESS DENIED," without ever changing their internal NPS (Negative Psyche System).

You can have the right code, but be with the wrong person. You can have the right password, but be in the wrong relationship. And you can have the right idea, but be in the wrong church.

Millionaire Job

10. And the Lord turned the captivity of Job, when he prayed for his friends; also the Lord gave Job twice as much as he had before.

11. Then came there unto him all his brethren, and all his sisters, and all they that had been of his acquaintance before, and did eat bread with him in his house; they bemoaned him and comforted him over all the evil that the Lord had brought upon him, every man also gave him a piece of money and every one an earring of gold.

12. ***So the Lord blessed the latter end of Job more than his beginning; for he had fourteen thousand sheep, six thousand camels, and a thousand yoke of oxen, and a thousand she asses.***

13. ***He had also seven sons and three daughters.***

14. And he called the name of the first and the name of the second, and the name of the third, Ker'en-hap'puch.

15. And in all the land were no women found so fair as the daughters of Job: and their father gave them inheritance among their brethren.

16. After this lived Job an hundred and forty years, and saw his sons, and his sons' sons, even four generations.

17. So Job died, being old and full of days.

—JOB 42: 10-17

Millionaire Status Principle #12

"The universe is ready to grant you your entire request, but you have the wrong software on your mental computer. You have to release, delete, forgive, let go, even get rid of certain things, before you receive on the computer "ACCESS GRANTED!"

If you have been programmed with a Negative Psychological Program, low inferiority, low esteem, pity-syndrome, a victimization complex, or a religious program which places your blessings in the "sweet bye and bye", and you go around blaming folks for your failures inside of yourself, you will see the blessing, but never experience it! You will see the miracle but it will pass you by.

Millionaire Status Principle #13

The miracle is in the right thought about yourself, others, money and prosperity. As a man THINKETH! Your primary enemies are between your ears! Cancel the negative self talk, negative events, and negative energy from manifesting in your future!

Gain the Consciousness of a Millionaire

Author, **Adrian Cooper**, in the book *Our Ultimate Reality,* stated that "imagination is one of the most powerful of all vibrations of energy in the universe." St. John 1:1 in the beginning was the word! Understand that the visible comes from the invisible world, therefore thoughts, migrations, energy produces all reality. Money is a symbol; your mind doesn't know the difference between real and fantasy. In the creation process you must go within or go without. All supply is within, it already exists within you, as a man thinketh so is his ultimate reality.

Millionaire Status suggests you meditate two to three hours a day to create the desired reality. Paint the picture in the corridors of your mind. You have the ability, the power, the creative genes of the maker to manifest new wealth, prosperity, money at any level. Tap into your hidden resources for the miracle is in the mind, Jesus never told you to lose your mind when you came into Kingdom, he said "renew your mind."

Become whatever you want to manifest. You desire to become a millionaire then gain the mentality (consciousness) of the rich and famous. Always be conscious that the color of freedom is neither black or white, it is green! You have to radiate, vibrate, and attract the desired results from within, as a man thinketh in his heart (visualization proceeds manifestation). If you can conceive it, you can have it!

As **Wallace Wattle** said in the masterpiece, *The Science of Getting Rich,* man is the apex of God's creation, a thinking center. God has to channel his desires through the mind of man. All thoughts and desires must be fashioned in your consciousness before it can exist in the world of form. Destroy the idea that money is evil. Your reality is a direct result of the way you think about a thing.

No Man Can Reach His Highest Pinnacle Being Poor.

A poverty mentality produces more poverty. You have to cleanse and chase all the poverty thinking, poverty images, poverty thieves, poverty music, someday over yonder when I die mentality and get rich quick schemes out of your mind. Beauty, opulence, abundance and prosperity are your birthright. Seize it with every breath and thought you take.

Thought is the only power which can produce tangible riches from formal substance. Every thought held in thinking substance, causes the creation of the form, in other words, faith is the substance of things hoped for, the evidence of things not seen. The seen comes from the unseen.

God will impregnate you, but God gives you the ability to birth your own vision.

"Thou shall meditate day and night, and then you shall have good success." **A miracle is not something that just happens. It is something that is created.** Every event, everything in your life, level of cash flow, level of relationships, level of happiness, yes you created it. We learn how to play with Play-Dough in kindergarten; you have the power to create worlds. Whatever you can conceive you can have. **As Zig Ziegler** coined the phrase "There is room at the top."

Plenty, abundances, unlimited possibilities are all around you in the universe ready for you to conceive as yours. It's your birth right to be rich. The reason you can't keep a 9 to 5 is because you have a genius within you that has the ability to make financially what you now make in 30 days, transfer in mentality to make in one day. Your vision has been too small, you are not waiting on God, divine intelligence is waiting on you to take the leap of faith.

Millionaire Status Principle #14

Have a burning desire, a definite time of manifesting your dream!

Nothing occurs by chance as a random occurrence, every single action or affect has an underlying cause. Proverbs 26:2 "the curse doesn't come without a cause." You become the cause and effect of your reality.

Prophet James Giles, one of my mentors and a master strategist in the field of human potential said that statisticians have documented that only 5% of society produces wealth. That means that 95% are consumers. Most people have no definite desire. They wander through life living hazardously instead of having a definite aim. You have to become conscious of where you are going or you'll end up where everyone else is on broken down lane, heading to bankruptcy court. Get a definite purpose in life, write it down, meditate day and night and birth the dream.

A country like Israel, smaller than any other nation, yet has produced the highest Gross National Product (GNP) but unlike the US, since 1991, it's still over 4 trillion dollars in debt. The current budget for federal spending is 1.5 trillion, but the government collects just a little over 1 trillion in taxes.

The answer to your dilemma you must have a power shift in the way of thinking, a power shift in three dimensions, relational, economically and spiritual to get the divine overflow blessings. You are trying to convince everybody about what you see. God said to Elijah, "If you see me, then you shall receive a double portion of my spirit." Your blessings are determined by who you are relational, economical, and spiritually connected to in this hour. Don't miss your divine appointment, predestine plan because the crowd have spiritual blindness and your family or kinfolk think you are crazy. Most millionaires had a touch of insanity.

This revelation will change whole cities, corporations, churches to have a complete turnaround in their finances by making a complete power shift in consciousness. Power shift is a shifting from the normal way of thinking. Wealth images, wealth vibrations, music, money symbols and prosperity thoughts must be imparted to your environment. Some places you can't go to with certain energy or certain relationships are too toxic to produce Kingdom. It may have worked in the past, but now you must shift to the new season. (Prophetic word 2006 January)

You began to think like **Einstein,** outside of the box. Think unlike the crowd. The showcase of the most millionaires is individuals like Edison whose teacher told him he was retarded, yet today the world is lit by the revelation of one man. George Washington Carver who, through one peanut, made over 100 products.

Out run, out hustle, out jump and most of all out think your competition. Take the risk to reach the dreams; life never remembers anyone who comes in second place. Primarily what's in the consciousness of an individual call leader of the business, president or prime minister of the ruling nation is transferred into the people under their rule.

Bishop Ellis spoke a prophetic word in the Atlanta conference, he said God is in the business of restoring the ruler ship of the patriarch in the human family, transferring authority through a male species. The co-ruler ship with a womb will echo this same vision to children, and each child becomes a generational channel of blessing.

A ruler is used to measure distance. The degree of obedience will determine the level of your rule. You will never rule with a slave mentality, trying to tip God instead of tithing or looking for a dime on the ground. Find your God assignment and be faithful regardless of what the crowd thinks.

Millionaire Status Principle #15

Any being, thought, philosophy that does not celebrate your assignment disqualify them or it from your life.

You can't go up the elevator until you let someone, some ideal off; you expect elevation, watch association.

Millionaire Status Principle #16

Consciousness creates everything, become consciousness of what you desire to create

People are buying groceries online, and companies are broadcasting advertisement internationally through broadband satellites, still many people are computer illiterate. Get in the traffic to attract wealth, the horse and buggy era is long gone!

Power Shift in Leadership Thinking!

As Business CEO Leaders and producers, it's imperative to keep abreast to the consumers needs, **and shift** with the changing in society. Most businesses go into bankruptcy due to not improving, not keeping their products own the cutting edge of change.

Look at the country of Japan, World War II, the US bombing of the countries, Hiroshima, Nagasaki. Sixty million citizens were blown away by an atomic nuclear bomb. Japan leadership has boldly established their country as a 21st Century universal leader in the field of high technology. They manufacture more goods and services throughout the world, their population suffers fewer abortions, few teens at risk, and their population GNP is higher than most third world nations.

Unfortunately, the US has large corporations like ENRON in bankruptcy. The US is running a budget deficit of nearly $500 billion dollars since President Ronald Reagan left office. President Clinton improved on foreign relations, and reduced the national deficit which marginally improved the economy since the early depression. Now President Bush launched America in the War against Terrorism without the support of other countries like Russia, China, Pakistan, Morocco, Germany, Canada, Belgium, New Zealand and Sweden.

Presently the US is still at war in Iraq and over 2000 US military soldier have been killed with more soldiers in route to Baghdad. The US has outsourced jobs to foreign nations leaving their own country with high unemployment. Twenty billion dollars was promised for the reconstruction of Iraq? The consciousness of leaders infiltrate down. The social status of most citizens are worse since the 60's due to leadership not making a paradigm shift but big government rules.

In our backyard, over 30 million Americans still live in poverty and the divorce rate has skyrocketed. Most crimes are crimes of survival and 10 million of those are African Americans.

It has been said that when good men stand back and do nothing Evil triumphs!

Millionaire Status Principle #17

Insanity is doing the same thing over and over but expecting new results. Economically you must shift.

Since the early 60's the American dollar has passed through the Korean community seven times; passed through the Asian community five times and only passed through the African community once. We are in a state of emergency. No longer do you have an American dream. If you don't change your thinking all you will wake up to is an American nightmare.

We must alter our spending, direct our investments, lose the "bling-bling" mentality and become producers and consume less. We have produced an instant get-rich-quick generation; there must be an altering of one's consciousness.

"Your mind is a sacred enclosure, nothing can enter harmful without your promotion!"

—Ralph Waldo Emerson

Mike Murdock said if your brain was unrattled it would take the entire Empire State Building to house it. It would take a complete year for the water of the Niagara Falls to cool down, and your brain could generate enough electricity to light up, for a year, a country the size of Iraq.

Millionaire Status Principle #18

The power to create worlds, new incomes and new inventions only lie behind your ears. Your greatest warfare is within!

Inside of you, not outside of you, is the storehouse of possibilities. Take control of your destiny today. Stop allowing situations, circumstances, conditions to imprison your God Gifts. So what if you made a mistake. Mistakes become stepping stones toward greatness. So what if you fell down, get back up! All through the Bible men fell down, but Hallelujah for the grace of God, they got up.

Stop tormenting yourself about what you did. Recognize why the blood of Jesus is so powerful! No one can understand how a black cow can eat green grass and make white milk. No one can refute how God takes a dark heart, apply red blood and make it whiter than snow! Out of all of your afflictions, you shall be turned from silver to gold.

Break out of a life style of debt, unfulfillment, sickness, gloom, depression, wake out of the coma of religion, have unlimited warm cash right hear and right now. As it is within so it is without!

Take up your bed of poverty and walk into prosperity! You can have it all right here and right now but you have to decide, definitely, what you want, when you want it and who you want to share it with.

Martin Luther King spoke, "All can be great, brightness starts by finding your gift and serving humanity. We all have a drum major instinct; to be out front leading the band, but you can't lead the band until you turn your back on the crowd!"

Jesus said, "I only do and speak those things that please the father." Jesus never received a Grammy or an Emmy. He never rcccived the Nobel Peace Prize, the Oscar or was recognized by the Who's Who of religionists of his day, and yet even if I had 10,000 tongues I still couldn't praise him enough.

James T. Watson a wonderful Pastor preached about how and when Jesus was a boy, he played with children making birds out of the sand. The only difference was, Jesus would place his birds on fences and they would fly away.

The highest praise goes to those who serve unselfishly without even recognition. To all the unsung heroes, continue to serve even in silence, your labor is not in vain. God sees your tears, he hears your fear. Sometimes your greatest hour is just after midnight. Weeping may endure for a night but joy cometh in the morning.

Millionaire Status Principle #19

Declare your own destiny! Stop allowing your past to define you, refine yourself!

Stop allowing folks to write your script. Act on your vision, ignite your faith, elevate your consciousness and stop looking out the windows of yesterday. Come in out of the rain of fear, set sail into a new tomorrow! Turn your back on the crowd of unbelief and manifest your dream today. Activate a dream goal daily, the journey of a thousand miles begins with one single step! Step a single step, even if you can't take two steps.

Serita Jakes revealed in her book ***The Princess Within***, that God gives you the permission to go beyond your past. She further states that Cinderella was so eager to obey her fairy Godmother; she left her beautiful shoes behind and fled to the ball. The question I propose is what beautiful thing, person, ideal, situation do you need to leave behind in order to obey and fulfill God's highest plan for your life? Just step away into destiny. What ever you give up, God replaces with something better.

Millionaire Status Principle #20

Embrace! Walk into the cockpit of your new season. Say goodbye to the old season. Stay in your FLOW…

You can't wear winter clothes in the summer season. Job 8:7 "though thy beginnings are small, thy latter end shall **greatly increase**." Job 36:11 "If you obey then you will spend your days in pleasure and your years in prosperity!"

Step away from people who don't believe in you. Step away from friends, relatives, old relationships, traditions of man and decide to change right here, right now! When one door closes, Angels open up the new doors called imagination to the miracles in the mind!

Fire the thieves in your mind that have been telling you lies. You can become the millionaire next door. Dennis Waitely, a leading motivator said, "If you think you can, then you can!"

Myles Monroe, church leader, stated that "The richest place in the Earth is the graveyard." A place of unfulfilled dreams, untapped energy, and unused powers.

The best selling author of**, *Unlimited Power*, Tony Robbins** takes it to the level where one's reality can be altered or changed if individuals will change their internal representation and self talk about themselves. Sometimes groups, companies, churches, ethnic minorities have a negative picture on the inside that continues to cycle in their reality.

This can account for the violence in certain communities where you see negative billboards; liquor stores and alcohol advertisements high crime and drive-by shootings. Negative stereotypes of women on billboards with cigarettes in their mouths have negative subliminal hidden messages. In other communities, suburban and rich areas, you don't see signs that reflect this negative barrage of character.

There is **Prosperity Energy**, prosperity vibration that have to be incorporated in the home of children, adults, schools, colleges and corporate environments to produce the right effects. The images in the mind will manifest in time. All reality is a manifestation of imagination! As a student of truth, as you meditate, your outward world of money, freedom, right relationship, perfect career will materialize.

Power Of Meditation

The Western society is a driven society. Most churches are like fast food restaurants, many have the get in get out mentality and you see a small faithful crew at the altars. The Eastern cultures are given to meditation, and the Bible speaks emphatically of the power of one's meditation, yet few practice this truth.

Millionaire Status Principle #21

For every cause there is an effect.
You can become the cause and the effect of your life.

Your own mentality determines what class you are in. No longer can we play the race card, minimizing our own responsibility to cultivate our own backyard!

Dr. Paul Yongi Cho, pastor of the fastest growing church in the nation. In understanding the laws of physics stated in his book, *Fourth Dimension,* "Everything visible originated in the invisible." Using the laws of vision and dreams, his membership went from a tent cathedral to well over 600,000 members. One can gain dominion over situations by operating in the language of the Holy Spirit, which are visions and dreams.

Diet, music effects on manifestations

Individual physiology, appetite, food and diet have to be altered to get in a certain meditative state to attract wealth. Your eating habits can negatively affect the outcome of the state of mind that will create wealth. Specifically getting in a meditative posture is quite a struggle if you just ate 5 pizza's and spaghetti meat balls just prior to your visualization and meditation hour. Fasting often will detox the body and give you a stronger clarity in thought.

Activate the Law of Cause and effect thru mediating day and night. Your Mind is the cause and the effect of all in your life!

It's recommended to play certain music to stimulate the neurological syntaxes, dendrites and connectors of the brain. Symphony music, like Beethoven or Mozart will heighten creative forces in the brain. The medulla will release a chemical reaction according to certain sounds, waves and energy. The sounds will trigger positive reactions in the brain. Sounds, tones, pitches all register in the brain creating emotions and certain moods that triggers positive or negative reactions in children. Its note worthy also those hard sounds, certain music sounds create violence and induce behaviors that dull the brain.

Music has been shown to stimulate brain function. The brain is quick to focus on it. Music automatically touches three of the four modalities by which the brain processes information. It is auditory, kinesthetic/tactile (movement), and tactual (elicits emotion). When the lyrics are made available in the printed form, music also taps the visual modality. Rhyming and rhythmic input taps into other areas of the brain. Music is perhaps the best medium to store content with an "emotional charge" that can be brought back long after the lesson is over. Songs, poems, rhymes, and raps thus become effective vehicles for long term and cumulative learning. Because of its well known impact on one's sense of well-being and other feelings, it is a strong medium for spiritual formation and expression.

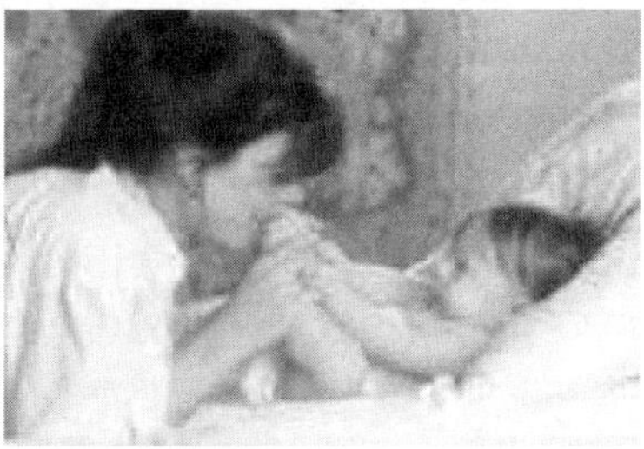

All of this suggests that even infants may benefit from exposure to classical music. Scientists have found that babies respond to changes in pitch. Very young infants brighten when you speak to them in a higher-pitched voice not because they understand your words but because they recognize a change in pitch and know it has been directed to them. Classical music -- with its rich variety of changes in pitch, tone and melody—can help to provide the varied stimuli a baby needs in order to thrive in the first year of life, when the brain develops faster than at any other time. At least one study has found that music can also aid in memory retrieval.

Wise teachers create an environment that encourages students to teach themselves. **Leonard Ray Frank**

PARENTS GUIDE TO RELEASING BRILLIANT MINDS

1. **Start as early as possible:** Start now. Whatever your child's age is - don't delay. If yours is a newborn, it is a perfect time to start. If your child is a teenager - it is not too late. As parents, it is our privilege, and our obligation to take care of our child's education. Now is the best time to start.

2. **Make it fun.** For children, learning is fun. What does a child do when he plays with his toys? He is diligently learning about his environment. If you observe a young child playing with his toys, you can see that when a child has completed learning all that he can learn from a toy, he tosses it aside, and looks for a new one! Keep it light and fun. This will ensure that your child grows to be a life long learner.

3. **You are your child's natural teacher**. No matter how many teachers your child has or will have in school and outside of school, you are his first and most important teacher. Take advantage of this and make sure you teach your child valuable lessons.

4. We all underestimate the ability of children to learn. When babies can't speak yet we don't know how much they can learn and how fast they learn. We don't know how much they can understand. But this is a very valuable period of time. At this time your child is learning his mother tongue. At this time your child has an amazing talent to recognize patterns. You can take advantage of this important period of time to teach your child many things related to language skills, like vocabulary, reading and more.

5. If you expose your child too many subjects and activities your child will show you what he is interested in. Then you can take advantage of his interest and relate other subjects to it. Let your child lead the way.

6. Children hate to be tested. Never test your child or it will stop being fun for him. Trust that whatever learning activity you are doing with your child is successful. Trust that your child is learning. Never doubt that. When it is the right time your child will show you how much he learned.

7. Children learn much faster than we adults do. If you want to keep your young child interested, you have to move at your child's speed - fast.

8. Your child's self confidence and self esteem are most important. Look for things to praise him for and avoid criticism. Every day, when your child goes to bed discuss the day's events and mention all the successes and achievements of the day. Get into the habit of doing this; it will make a big difference in your child's confidence.

9. Teach your child to set goals early on. Set yearly, monthly, weekly and daily goals. Teach your child how to put together a plan, and how to change the plan when it is necessary. At the end of the year celebrate the child's achievements. Make sure your child knows how successful he is.

10. Make sure your child knows that it's OK to make mistakes. It's OK to try and fail. Failure is just a learning opportunity, a signal to try a different way. A child that knows this will not be discouraged or give up. A child that knows this lesson will keep a healthy self esteem and confidence in spite of occasional set backs.

The more you teach your child, the stronger the bond between you. As you watch your child develop, succeed and meet his own goals, the memories you are creating together will turn into the dearest memories in your child's life, and in your own.

Increase Personal Magnetism

Millionaire Status philosophically recognizes that your mind is the exact duplicate of the nucleus of an atom similar to the molecular structure of our DNA which is the building blocks of life. Life therefore starts not only at the concept of the womb but new life starts at the conception of thought.

Millionaire Status Principle #22

THOUGHTS + WAVES +ENERGY+SOUNDS=Manifestation
You can manifest what you want by working with energy and magnetism

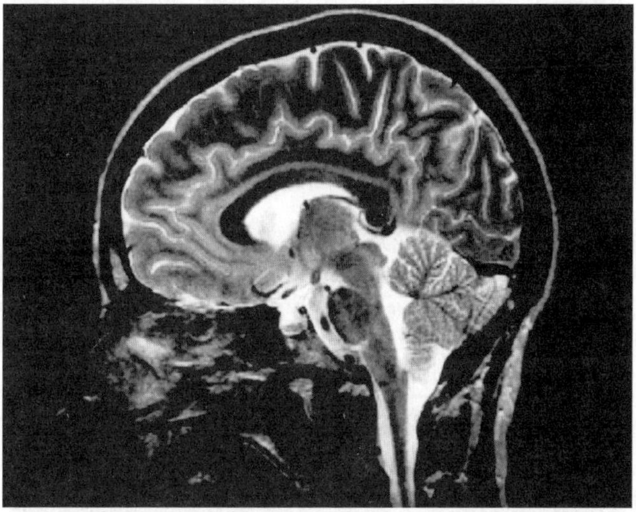

The Mind is your personal Broadcasting station, tune in to the channel of riches, increase the frequency, deliberately manifest at will, the mind has 40,000 to 50,000 thoughts a day, when you harness 1000 to 2000 of those daily thoughts to a specific goal , it will manifest, the MAGIC Is WITHIN!

The divine has only one entry in the earth, thru the birth canal of all substance, man's unlimited imagination!

Prophet Israel

The most powerful way to develop creativity in your students is to be a role model. Children develop creativity not when you tell them to, but when you show them.

Robert J. Sternberg in ***How To Develop Student Creativity***

We learn....

10% of what we read.

20% of what we hear.

30% of what we see.
50% of what we both see and hear.
70% of what is discussed with others
80% of what we experience
95% of what we teach
William Glasser

Einstein noted, "Nothing has power over me except that which I give through my conscious thought." He also discovered that certain brain syntaxes lose their ability to send and receive messages due to one not knowing how to heighten his mental awareness. The Bible speaks that, "In the beginning was the word." Before there was the word; there was energy, before energy there was thought!

Millionaire Status Principle #23

Your mind will manifest anything at the level, time, and degree of rotation in your meditative thought. Meditation must precede manifestation of any demonstration of money.

The only difference between gold and silver is the amount of rotation fusion of the element that surrounds the nucleus transforming its nature.

Place the symbol of wealth, rich, elegance, and develop a millionaire consciousness within and find the magician is within you!

Millionaire Status Principle #24

Increase Your Capacity To Hold Millions By Reading About Millionaires!

There is tremendous wealth of information in the , Millionaire Magazine, Oprah Magazine, Essence, Black Enterprises, Forbes, Fortune 500, and Money Magazine to prosper your soul and renew your mind through reading wealth materials. It is said that the average person only reads one book a year!

This has nothing to do with saying abbra cadabra or rubbing bottles, or shouting money cometh or anointing with oil until Christmas come. People in churches have a mild form of spiritual dyslexia, and these thinking errors have not been mixed with truth.

Kings and Queens live by principles of their kingdom. They establish there jurisdiction of rule, and are surrounded by rich royal estates managed by loyal employees

A king lives by the principles of his kingdom, Proverbs 4:7 states, "Wisdom is the principal thing, get wisdom!" Solomon's wisdom excelled any king's of the East countries. Queen Sheba paid Solomon over $3 million for his gene pool, (royal bounty). She traveled out of her country, Ethiopia to find the man who had the same imagination as hers. She was amazed by King Solomon's wealth consciousness, impressed by his kingdom and intelligence. His palace was surrounded with gold and servants who dressed in royalty. His affluence literally took her breath away. When you walk in a room it should take your breath away!

Mastering the Creation process

These principles, when they are applied, will manifest into tangible substance only when they govern your every thought, concentration and daily meditation. Without these universal principals you will remain in a comatose environment. Debt will continue to increase, fear will grip your heart and depression will invade your life as winter invades spring. Consciousness is everything! As a man thinketh!

You want to change as **David Schwartz** said "There is a magic in thinking big." In the Bible be like Joseph, dream yourself from the pits of life to the million dollar mansion and get in the place where you deserve it! Life owes no man anything. Life gives to the giver and takes from the taker.

U. S. Andersen said, "The one mind in which we all live contains an infinite number of possibilities, all capable of manifesting in space and time, for it is attracted by an irresistible and immutable law called, the law of attraction. (you attract what you think)

Master the laws that govern the UNIVERSE!

Unless you studied **Newton's Theory laws of aerodynamics** in physics, one will grasp that it's humanly impossible. Those who master the laws of aerodynamics understand what makes a 20,000 ton airplane stay in flight.

A child will struggle in subtraction because he has not mastered the laws of addition. In thought you have to matriculate from the level of adding to subtracting, to decimals, percentages, fractions, multiplication, algebra, calculus, geometric and then move to understanding the trigonometry of life. Move on to understanding approximations, linear math, laws of physics and awake the genius brain within you. Persevere to solving the Pythagorean Theorem.

Some equations in life you start out thinking will him or her or a new relationship, career move and location change will add to your life but prophetically you need to be realigned in understanding some places you can't go until you subtract, divide and remove certain entities from you, your life and most definitely from your mind!

How can you go to the next dimension in partnership with those who are comfortable at ground level? You can't place wings on a bird that doesn't want to fly! Get comfortable with your own level of greatness, excel, redefine and refine and motivate yourself! Stop allowing your past to terminate your future. As renowned author **T.D. Jakes often say, "If life gives you a lemon, then baby make lemonade."**

Millionaire Status Principle #25

Learn the laws which govern whatever you desire to manifest, then you will walk above water!

Wallace Wattles in his book entitled, *The Science of Getting Rich,* stated that there is an exact science of getting rich. Living prosperous is an exact science like algebra and arithmetic. When certain laws are activated the acquisition of wealth will be realized.

Big business conglomerates have put the mom's and pops stores out of business, society is witnessing the downsizing of major corporations and the paradigm has shift. It is time for you, the individual, to have a power shift in consciousness and relationships. Some levels in life you can't get to with certain people and certain jobs are becoming obsolete. You must realize inside of you is a million dollar idea ready to be released to the earth. You have got to go to the next level!

At this moment, this word you are reading has the possibilities of manifesting. If you believe, you can change your income, change your place of dwelling and alter your thinking. Come into the consciousness of a millionaire.

U.S. Andersen in the book, *Three Magic Words,* gives you to know that the most powerful instrument in the universe is within man, the mind of man is the mind of the maker.

Man being the Apex of God's Creation, your imagination is creation. Jesus said in St. Luke 17:21, "The Kingdom is within." I like what **Prophet Jordan at Zoë Ministries prophesied, "Go within or go without**." When there is a need always goes within in the manifestation process. You are called not to wait on the rapture but to manifest Kingdom in the earth.

The heavens are God's throne. The heavens represent the mind, the consciousness of man. Heaven is not some place outside of you, it is within man, and you have to tap inside of your hidden resources to renew the mind! Get all the junk out of your mind, junk of poverty, junk of some one is against you and the junk of thinking some one is the cause of your problems. Resentment and unforgivingness is the cause of your problem. Stop being a mental junkie. As a man thinketh in his heart so is he. You manifest what you think!

Millionaire Status is solely a philosophy of living on practical keys and skills on how to manifest whatever you desire in life. It is not just about a tangible substance called money, which is paper. You desire more money, create a service for humanity, a vacuum to attract new money and then create a consciousness of wealth. You desire better health then meditate on a health. You desire right relationships then meditate on right relationships.

Increase demands on yourself

If the vehicle you are riding in life is only producing $5000 a month and you desire to move to $10,000 monthly or daily then consider changing vehicles. God told Moses, "Stop praying raise up the rod which is in your hand." Sometimes we simply need to examine what's in our hand! Make friends with the rich! The rich begets the rich. Jesus said "The poor you will always have." Just don't you be one. Poor people cannot build kingdom.

Take out all the negative sabotaging images, resentment, and bitterness of people who mistreated you. Walk in divine love. Stop thinking that white people or black people are against you. Out of one blood made him all nations.

Develop a millionaire consciousness. Vibrate, radiate, dress up for where you are going, not where you been. Stop reminding yourself of past failures, broken dreams and bad relationships. If it didn't work out then it was not ordained in the first place. Purge yourself from it, from him or her, from the last negative episode and stop reliving the past. The only thing good about the good old days is that they are old and gone!

Purge yourself from any negative talk, toxic relationship, negative people, and gossiping friends. Deliver yourself from their company. If you don't like what is on your screen of life, then stop downloading the negative demeaning sabotaging images! Speak and think well over yourself and all in your world.

The earth is man's throne to rule. All the enemies within your mind are to become our footstool in the earth. You are called to own properties, own cities and own companies. You are designed to be an entrepreneur!

St. Luke 19:17 "And he said unto him, well thou good servant, because thou hast been faithful in a very little, have thou authority over ten cities."

Napoleon Hill said, "Think and grow rich," think yourself out of poverty, think yourself out of a renter mentality, think yourself out of depression, think yourself into a lifestyle of the rich and famous. Forgive and let the past go. Stop waiting on the "sweet bye and bye" and cash in on the sweet now and now! No more crumbs for me!

Deepak Chopra, stated in the book, The Seven Laws of Success, that in order to achieve our optimal vibration, we must surrender to our own Divinity, we must let go of all self-limiting, ego driven thoughts and instead surrender to a higher power, a Divine order, that says we're all one. Jesus said," Father make them one even as I and you are one." Jesus' prayer was that all become one with the Father of the Universe! One in thought, one in physical, one in mind that is why we understand the sole purpose of meditation is not to get but become!

I am that I am. I am, God's first name, what you add to it comes behind it. I am rich, I am healthy, I am wealthy, and I am that I am! Stop speaking what you have, speak the desired results. Mark 11:23 "Whatsoever you say and believe when you pray you shall have it!" You are snared by the words of you mouth. Life and death are in the power of the tongue. The four laws of creativity, you have to see it, taste it, feel it, and become it! Change your self talk and internal representations. Speak yourself into your Millionaire Status! You don't have to wait until the sweet bye and bye, to actualize your dreams in the now and now!

Break out of the comfort zone of poverty; stretch yourself into the zones of miracles, where whatever is in mind manifests in time. You must understand how to become the Thinker of your own universe.

In Genesis 1:26 Eloim prophesy that you, regardless of the color at birth, or what society dictates your worth, you have been genetically engineered and wired up with intrinsic powers to produce prosperity through your mental forces. Get out of religion; get back to God's original design for your life, where dominion is at your fingertips and prosperity is your birthright!

Apostle Paul coined the phrase "Let this mind be in you that was in Christ Jesus." Many have this belief that Jesus Christ was a broken down, poverty stricken; lay away installment plan, bankrupt savior.

Jesus was a millionaire. Jesus recruited a company of rich men to revolutionize change the world. Jesus was a powerful visionary, who took his vision from a manger to become a universal icon. The King of Glory was not a broken down derelict and certainly not poor. He walked above matter. He raised dead things; he fed 25,000 people with five loaves of bread and two fish; he commanded the earth to stand still; he screwed the stars in their silver sockets of glory; he hung the moon by night and hung the sun by day. With his teardrops he made oceans and seas and mastered all the laws of the universe. You have to master self. Master your gift and cultivate it to where it will go from living room to Wall Street.

Jesus had a millionaire prosperous background. He matriculated down from fourteen generations. In his genetics code were Kings like David, rulers like Solomon, prime ministers like Joseph, and fathers of Nations like Abraham. He was born in an insignificant manger, raised to a mighty significant person that at the sound of his name nation's trembled, even at birth wise men presented him with the richest of gifts, gold, frankincense and myrrh. Jesus obviously had no problem with money, he told his disciples to make friends with the rich, but feed the poor.

Take a prophetic look at the friends around you; they are a snapshot of your future. The poor begets the poor. Make friends with the rich. The bible states that a poor man's wisdom is never heard.

In Jesus' ministry, he never killed a chicken, never wrote a grant, and never had a bake sale or a car wash to raise money for the church. Jesus was a master manifester. When taxes had to be paid, he directed Peter to fish at a lake with golden coins in his mouth. Jesus first crusade was preaching from one of his disciple Yacht. It's not a part of your divine nature to be poor; you have an ever present supply of prosperity all around you. Infinite substance is manifesting in you right now.

Millionaire Status Principle #26

Impress daily positive affirmations and mentally exact forms, dimensions, colorful pictures of your desires and they will manifest.

You're only limited by the way you think. Renew your mind! There are no limits to your manifestations. Your mind is a center of divine operation and contains wealth within the invisible forces of the universe. Whatever has not manifested is not in your imagination.

It is absurd to see that the percentage of people on the planet creating and producing wealth is only 5%. Seventy five percent of inner cities youths are locked into an American nightmare thinking that the sports is their escape mechanism, when only 1% out of a 1000 make it.

Dare to be different

Yes there are millions of possibilities to be! Dare to be different. Inspire your self to be like a Michael Jordan, better yet become a golfer like a Tiger Woods or inspire to preach like Apostle Paul, motivate thyself to mother like Hannah, raise a prophet like a Samuel, all have gifts to offer humanity, govern like Deborah, communicate like Oprah Winfrey or compute like a Bill Gates.

But don't stop there, create and produce like Steven Spielberg; act like Halle Berry; run like Deion Sanders and don't stop there. Become an expert In journalism like Barbara Walters or excel in comedy like Chris Rock; a rapper like Kanya West; a powerful attorney like Johnny Cochran; a heavyweight boxing champion of the world like Muhammad Ali; a manager like Lee Iacocca and love like a Mother Theresa. **Cultivate your gift. Elevate and make yourself in demand. Celebrate thyself, don't let anyone rain on your parade! Leave your footprints in the sand.**

Become conscious of why the Divinity manifested you in the earth. Realize God only made one choice and God never made junk. You are the spitting image of a masterpiece in the making. You made mistakes get back on the court of life and dance again! Realize the dynamic nitroglycerin inexhaustible infinite potentials within you.

As **Orison Marden, in** the book entitled, *Miracle of Right Thought* stated

"No man has a right, unless he cannot help himself, to remain where he will be constantly subjected to the cramping, ambition blighting influences and great temptations of poverty." His self respect demands that he should get out of such an environment. It is his duty to put himself in a position of dignity and independence, where he will not be liable at any moment to be a burden to his friends in case of sickness or other emergencies.

Linda Georgian in her writings says Angels look for openings in our consciousness. They slip into our thoughts and dreams making the millions of impossibilities creating new realities!

Bishop Jordan prophecy's that you have to become the push and the pull to your own dreams, dream big dreams. God cannot fulfill small receipts. Attempt something so big that the only way you will succeed is only when all the authority in the universe is backing you up and you will win! Dare to be different, dream again!

Stop complaining what should have been. Stop being frustrated about not having shoes, until you see the boy running down the street with no feet. Jesus could have complained about being betrayed by Judas, but without the betrayals there would be no resurrections and new beginnings! Get out of the grave of yesterday, loose yourself from the tomb of hopelessness, set your sail away from the intoxicating beverage of sadness and dream again. There's a new wave of blessings coming into your shore.

Find the Genius in You

Many can aspire to become another Plato, Socrates or paint like Michael Angelo; write like Maya Angelou; compose like Beethoven; sing like Marian Anderson or develop vaccines like Jonas Salk. Everyone was birth from eternity with the seeds of greatness; you don't have to be a clone of anyone. Find your greatness, market, manufacture and maximize it. The Bible says it will cause you to walk in places with Kings and Queens. Stop wasting time, mine your own mind, fire and hire yourself and create from within! Any burning bush will do, shine right where you were assigned!

Grasp opportunities!

Eastern philosopher, **Paramahamsa Yogananda** said "Success, prosperity in life does not altogether depend on ability or training, it also depends on your determination to grasp opportunities that are presented to you, and opportunities in life come by creation, not by chance."

Society has black millionaires, Hispanic millionaires, European millionaires, Jewish, Asians, Japanese, German, Russian and Native American millionaires who have mastered the laws; persevered against the odds obtaining and exceeds plateaus, ridiculous lifestyle of the rich and famous, while others only live in a survival mode and fantasy about it.

Many have a belief system that only operates when they die. This belief system rules them and 95% of them are one check away from the welfare roll. They still have a renter and bling-bling mentality, its time to shift.

You were endowed with the mind of the predecessor of the universe. It doesn't matter what side of the railroad you were born on, it only matters if you decide to download the unlimited wealth possibilities within to change the world.

Whoever thought today we would be flying in jets at the speed of light; whoever thought we would be riding in Rolls Royce and whoever dreamed man would be landing on Mars? Utilize the eleven thousand kilowatts of power between your ears and find the vaccine to cure the AIDS virus.

Millionaire Status is certainly not a get rich quick scheme, or a money cometh manual. This is the quantum leap into creating worlds. What lies behind you is not as important as to what lies within you, acres of untapped potentials, powers, inventions and creations. Stop listening to the crowd, push your way through the doubters and fulfill the millions of dreams the father infused within you. As it is within, so it is without. When the children of Israel left Egypt, God declared unto them, you shall not go empty!

There were no airplanes in year one. It was a practical joke to think of flying in an airplane. Past generations couldn't conceive the possibility of the ideal, yet it came to pass.

Find Balance Bloom Where You Are Planted

The key to successful life, business, family, organization is in this final key, Balance. Use the hand that the universe has dealt you and stop trading your cards in for another deck. Everybody has gifts and talents that need to be cultivated.

Don't fantasize, pray and recognize the level of your greatness. God can elevate you as you shine in the darkness, whether it's a mother taking care of her children, father who is a mechanic, child who works at the diner, shine where you were planted.

Don't lose a marriage in search of a dream; don't lose your children in search of another hot deal; don't lose your husband comparing him to the Jones or wife to some "hotty" on the big screen. Get in a quiet place and hear God. Make sure you spend time alone in the furnace of miracles called solitude, prayer, meditation, balance your life goals and build solid relationships. Cultivate your own garden and grow it well.

Acres of Diamonds, the book where the man lost his farm full of acres of diamonds in search of success, when in reality; success was in his own backyard. Don't chase a dream that God didn't place in you.

Acres of Diamonds are within you. How many divorces, alcoholics, cocaine addicts quit the game of life were caused by self search; in search of a dream, in search of riches, when riches stared them in the face. Take time to smell the roses. True riches are within! Serve the people you were called to serve. Bloom where you were planted, cultivate, and renovate your relationships each year.

Be faithful where you are; be faithful with who you are and who you're with; in that family; organization and team. Instead of complaining about your race, take your place, rest the discrimination case, complete not compete, celebrate not tolerate, turn silver into gold! STARS ONLY SHINE IN DARKNESS!

Millionaire Status Wisdom Keys will catapult you from a man to a Superman empowering you to demonstrate all endowed within you. Right here and now, make a definite purpose decision to stop allowing man's religion, bad relationships, and systems to sabotage the ordained plan in which you were ordained to walk in affluence, influence and divine intelligence.

Today make a decision to consciously make a paradigm shift from the old way of thinking, to the new order, the Manifestation stage, where all desired dreams become reality.

Regardless of your color at birth many value your worth and awake the genius abilities within. Come into a realm, awareness, knowledge and understanding the Kingdom to unleash your astronomical untapped potentials and powers that were deposited in you.

ACTIVATE TODAY!

You have now purchased the golden key and you will manifest at the level of Millionaire Status where wealth, affluence, influence and the lifestyle of the rich and famous will be at your fingertips. Human potential studies suggest it takes 60 days of repetitive study to affirm a new habit. You have to become conscious of whatever it is you desire. Become it! Taste it! Feel the vibrations of it! Radiate it! And it will become you in 60 days. Get ready to shift to the new paradigm and experience wealth, health and prosperity in all levels of life!

Millionaires have a definite plan!

Start your journey of discovery today, don't procrastinate. The future belongs to those who take charge of their destiny. Know the laws which govern the universe, practice them daily, and comprehend with all faith.

"And hath made us Kings and Priests unto God and his father, to him be glory and dominion, forever and ever. Amen" Rev 1:6

These are things to come; a Revelation of the future. God is about to change your present, erasing your past, and ignite your destiny through this word. He is about to expand you, enlarging your territory and stretch your borders. We are at the closing of one Era and the opening of a complete new Epoch. A complete new generation is emerging; it's time to go to the NEXT LEVEL. The pages of this book will cause you to see the depths, lengths, the height and the breadth of Christ. His kingdom, the royalty you have been ordained to walk in and enjoy and the wealth has been decreed for you to leave as a legacy for the next generation.

Millionaire Status Principle #27

You respond to God according to your revelation, belief system and upbringing of him. You need a fresh revelation of the riches and the glories of the kingdom.

Prophetically, God is transitioning his church from the systems of man to enter into Kingdom! Man has plans but God is establishing purpose. God is orchestrating a complete take over.

Josh 6: 13 "And it came to pass when Joshua was by Jericho, that a he lifted up his eyes and looked and there stood a man over against him with a sword drawn in his hand, and Joshua went unto him and said unto him, and said Art thy for us, or for our adversaries? And he said Nay, but as the Captain of the Host of the Lord, I am now come, Joshua fell on his face to the earth and asked, what faith it lord unto his servant?"

There is a new glory that is about to be revealed that you have yet to experience. This word is designed to loose the seals on your life, enabling you to fulfill the volumes and the archives written on you in eternity. You were a word in the presence of God until God said let it be! You will learn to activate your creative genes and operate in kingdom principles and laws, which govern the universe to create the very world, God ordained you to live in. You are about to experience God in the riches of his KINGDOM, the royalty of his court and the splendor of his glory; he is now extending his royal scepter unto you.

"In the beginning God created the heavens and the earth and the earth was without form and void. And darkness was upon the face of the deep, and the spirit of God moved upon the face of the waters, and God said let there be light!"

God almighty blesses thee, and makes thee fruitful, and he gives thee the blessings of Abraham Gen 28: 3-4

- Samuel 2:7 The Lord maketh Poor and Maketh rich, he bringeth low and lifted up, lie raiseth up the poor out of the dust and lifted up the beggar from the dunghill, to set them among princes, and to make inherit the throne of His glory.
- Isaiah 45:3 and I will go before you, and make the crooked places straight; I will break in pieces the gates of brass, and cut in sunder the bars of iron. And I will give thee the treasures of darkness and the hidden treasures of

the secret places. Places in which you could not access, you are about to access, there is about to be given. You have keys to unlock all doors; wealth is being transferred to its rightful place!

- Esth 10:5 For Mordecai the Jew was next unto King Ahasuerus and great among the Jews, and accepted of the multitude of his brethren, seeking the wealth of his people and speaking peace unto his seed.
- Job 22:2 1 acquaint now thyself with him, and are at peace and good shall come unto thee.
- Job 22:24 then shalt thou lay up GOLD as dust, and the GOLD of Ophir as the stones of the brook, yea the almighty shall be thy defense, and thou shalt have plenty of silver.
- Psalm 66: 12 But thou broughtest us out into a wealthy place . . .
- Psalm 35:27 let the Lord is magnified, which had pleasure in the Prosperity of his servants.
- Ecc 10: 18 Money answers all things

Money is not designed to sustain you. Divine intelligencc, the God power within you, is your source. The substance of money doesn't determine your value or worth, money is a medium of exchange in the earth realm. God intended for you to develop your spirit man to sustain you through every season of life, by applying the laws that govern the universe, by grasping infinite wisdom, and walking in the infinite intelligence of God's wealth, money, and prosperity will overtake you. You will have an infinite unending supply of security in all realms of life.

Power of Money

Your money must make money. You were not designed to work for money; money was designed to work for you. That's why you must start early to accumulate wealth. Start early operating on cash only sales! God is a God of cash as well as credit.

Don't get caught in the credit card scam. Watch your spending habits, videos and entertainment daily. Have a budget! Tell your money where to go and not ask where it went at the end of the month.

Read money magazines, Fortune 500, Money, Success magazine, Entrepreneur magazines and magazines studying on how to open franchises. As a student, study the market, what's in demand today, may not be in demands for tomorrow.

ECC 10: 19 Speaks boldly to the believer that money answers all things. "By much slothfulness the building decay, and thru the idleness of the hands the house dropped thru, a feast is made for laughter, and wine maketh merry, but money answerth all things."

Hosea, the prophet reminds us that the Church had been destroyed due to the lack of knowledge. This book will equip you with revelation knowledge of wealth and money!

Money is the world's God. Money is designed to serve you; it must become a servant of demonstrating kingdom in the earth. **You have astronomical abilities, wisdom and gifts to take the world's God and make it your servant and to fulfill the countless dreams and visions pregnant within you.**

Millionaire Status Principle #28

God never went outside himself to fulfill anything, he looked within himself and said, "LET THERE BE."

Economically every person, even the nation has been under a direct financial frontal attack and its time we attack back with arsenal of angels, wisdom and prophetic insight. Now! Let's Wage war against the assault upon our predestined original purpose of generating wealth and leave a legacy of affluence to the next generation.

Millionaire Status Principle #29

Money doesn't make a man successful; it's the thinking of the man. Napoleon Hill coined it, "You must think and grow rich and learn how to generate capital to generate generational wealth.

ECC 10: 19 "But money answereth all things!"

ST. MATT 17:27 "Not withstanding, lest we should offend them, go to the sea, and cast in a hook, and take up the fish that first cometh up, and when thou hast open his mouth, thou shalt find a piece of money, that take and give unto them for me."

Philip Danforth Armour 1832- 1901

Returning home from the gold rush at twenty-four with several thousand dollars in his pocket, he turned to meat packing, and near the end of the Civil War he found a way to turn meat into gold, selling pork futures at forty dollars a barrel and then buying the pork for eighteen dollars after the Confederacy collapsed. With the nearly two-million-dollar profit that resulted, he built Armour & Company. He was one of the first to bring hogs to Chicago for slaughter at his own plant, and he cut waste by using leftovers to make glue, soap, and fertilizer. Hurt by the 1898-99 meat scandals that inspired Upton Sinclair's *The Jungle, he gave away perhaps half his fortune.*

Mark Hopkins 1813-1878

A quiet, reasonable man, he does not jump out of the history books as do his partners in the Central Pacific Railroad, but as its treasurer, working behind the scenes, he provided the levelheaded business sense that made the other three extremely rich: Two are on this list; the other, Charles Crocker, missed by only two places. Lured to California by gold, he soon figured he could make more money supplying miners and opened an iron and hardware store with Collis Huntington (No. 28). It was in the apartment over that store that an engineer persuaded the soon-to-be big Four to finance what would become the Central Pacific.

Job 42: 10-17

10. And the Lord turned the captivity of Job, when he prayed for his friends; also the Lord gave Job twice as much as he had before.

11. Then came there unto him all his brethren, and all his sisters, and all they that had been of his acquaintance before, and did eat bread with him in his house; they bemoaned him and comforted him over all the evil that the Lord had brought upon him, every man also gave him a piece of money and every one an earring of gold.

12. So the Lord blessed the latter end of Job more than his beginning; for he had fourteen thousand sheep, six thousand camels, and a thousand yoke of oxen, and a thousand she asses.

13. He had also seven sons and three daughters.

14. And he called the name of the and the name of the second, and the name of the third, Ker'en-hap'puch.

15. And in all the land were no women found so fair as the daughters of Job: and their father gave them inheritance among their brethren.

16. After this lived Job an hundred and forty years, and saw his sons, and his sons' sons, even four generations.

17. So Job died, being old and full of days.

John Pierpont Morgan 1837-1913

A famously imposing man, he showed his mettle at twenty-one, when he enraged his employers by buying a ship load of coffee without their authorization and then turned out to have sold the entire cargo at a healthy profit before it had even arrived at the dock. He was born rich, but he made his own fortune along with a reputation as the most powerful, dependable, and forthright man on Wall Street, underwriting the creation of such corporations as General Electric, International Harvester, and U.S. Steel. He was actually powerful far out of proportion to his wealth; during the Panic of 1907 he averted national disaster by raising twenty-five million dollars in fifteen minutes and single-handedly keeping the Stock Exchange from closing early. Within twelve hours of his death, while vacationing in Rome, his family received 3,698 telegrams of condolence.

Paul G. Allen 1953-

This whiz kid was blessed with both an interest in computers and being a high school classmate of Bill Gates (No. 5) though perhaps Gates was blessed with being his classmate too. He dropped out of Washington State to go to work for Honeywell before joining Gates in 1975 to found Microsoft, which took off in the early 1980's. He retired from active involvement in Microsoft in 1983 after learning that he had Hodgkin's disease, from which he later recovered, but he is still the company's second-largest stockholder. He also owns, among other things, the Seattle Seahawks football team and the Portland Trail Blazers basketball team.

Biblical Economics

Biblical Economics is a strategic tool to move you into Kingdom riches thereby rebuking the generational curses and cycles of poverty and debt from your life. By learning and activating Kingdom principles and governing your life according to these wisdom keys you will establish generational wealth to leave a legacy of wealth for the next generation. God has declared you to be RICH! Receive a clear word and clarity on the God perspective of wealth and money.

Millionaire Status Principle #30

You will become your most dominant thought!

Pursuit the Kingdom within you, Jesus said, "Seek ye first the kingdom and all these other things shall be added to you!" The Kingdom is the rule and reign of Christ in all realms of your life and being obedient to the covenant of God. In Genesis 1, it states God created man in His image, to have, to ring, to naught the works of darkness and exercise dominion over his environment. You have the power to change your reality, change your conditions, and create new realities through the divine nature of the one who created you. Stop limiting your God powers . . .

Most people have been in poverty due to religious ignorance. We hope to inspire you to become the millionaire in the pew! Realize God created you in His image to have DOMINION in all realms of your life. Money has been the world's God, our role is to take the world's God and make it the church servant.

God has not destined you to be poor. Religious tradition has reduced the man God created to be a Ruler, a Master, a C.E.O., a King, to a beggar. God genetically designed you with the same creative dreams, ideals, wisdom, and imagination that can produce a millionaire lifestyle. We prophesy that the day will come where the church does not depend on government grants and bank loans but acquire things by CASH!

In order for a new cycle to start an old cycle must end!

The tradition of man has distorted the original ROYAL RICH Image of the kingdom by having rummage sales, car washes, bake sales and chicken dinners. God has only one program to enrich you. **The kingdom principal of tithing and giving offerings.** We are to be in covenant with him and with our church.

Man was ordained to be the overseer and C.E.O. of the earth. Adam lost his place, misplaced the woman, displaced the family and we still have not rebounded from the original fall. Instead of ruling with the Royal Scepter, Adam got caught up in flesh and exchanged his dominion destiny because of the seductive nature of a woman. We must return to first things, the law of dominion. We are called to dominate our domain.

The glory of God is not noise, it's the tangible evidences manifested blessings in your life!

Warning! This revelation will cause an attack. Your money angel is about to send supernatural abundant supplies your way to establish the kingdom. New moneymaking, wealth-activating ideals are filling your consciousness. You will become the next millionaire in the pew!

There is a Covenant of prosperity. God said he would give us the ability to get wealth to establish the covenant in the earth. Knowledge of the covenants is of uttermost importance to the believer's Wealth and Success in the earth. My people have been destroyed because of the lack of knowledge!

Poverty is a curse, prosperity is a blessing!

In this book, you will receive a fresh Revelation, insight and skillful knowledge in regards to the perspective of how God thinks about money. Wealth Prosperity will deliver you, your church, and family from the CURSE of POVERTY and bring you into the COVENANTS OF BLESSINGS and grant you the ability to become debt free, own your own business, purchase your own franchise and transfer the wealth to the church!

God is in direct agreement to BLESS YOU! Examine where you have wasted money and wasted energy then redirect the resources without being in bondage to man. God created you to represent all that he is.
God is about to turn all your Ishmael's into gold mines!

Genesis 12: 1-2, Now the Lord had said unto Abram. Get thee out of thy country, (from a certain mindset) and from thy kin folks, and from thy father's house (tradition), unto a land that I will show thee, and I will make of thee a great nation, I will bless thee, and I will make thy name great. And thou shalt be a blessing. God's highest desire is to make you a channel of blessings. No one can withstand the full glory of God.
Therefore you are progressively taken from one level to another realm to glory!

Wealth Meditation

Confess now: Everyday in every way I am coming into permanent unending and unlimited inexhaustible riches of the kingdom. Now I see prosperity, wealth, health, and security flow in all realms of my life, business, family and community. Abundance is all around me. I dream wealth dreams, I see myself wealthy, and I feel wealthy, I am wealthy. My wealth causes others to become wealthy. I am now a channel of prosperity, love, and extend to all that come into my world. Thy kingdom comes!

First Mandate of Man

This **1st Commission** was given and must be fulfilled before we can effectively disciple the nations; the church has to be disciple in kingdom finances and economics, then we progressively disciple the community. Proverbs 4:7 "admonish us to get wisdom." Wisdom is a principle that PRINCES' LIVE by that are created and govern the universe.

Wisdom transfer to wealth

Our wisdom will reflect in our lifestyle. There is a king, and there is a kingdom, then there are those subject to the king's authority and decreed. We are here to kick in the very gates of hell, occupy, preside, rule, reign in his stead as ambassadors of power and influencing every sphere of man.

Millionaire Status Principle #31

Never underestimate your abilities, and over estimate others abilities, make your self in demand! Stir up your gifts.

And God said **Let us make man in our image,** after our likeliness: and let them have dominion over the fish of the sea, and over the fowl of the air, and over the cattle, and over all the earth, and over every creeping thing that creepeth upon the earth. God is a creator, so man was ordained to create. When you came into the kingdom, no one told you to lose your mind. You were told to renew your mind.

Your mind is the incubator of purpose!

This is why the scripture says; "Let this mind be in you that was in Jesus Christ!" A creative mind, intelligence mind, we need the mind of the master. **The battlefield happens between your ears.** Most people only use 5% of their brainpower. If you learn to exercise the other 95% of your brain power you would astonish yourself, possibly learn 5 different languages and earn 8 different degrees. Most people waste 95% of their brainpower on negative demeaning unproductive thoughts. Thoughts are powerful, they become things. **The thieves of your destiny are between your ears.**

Mind-power

Most people will astound themselves of what they would accomplish in life if they start utilizing **the other** 95% of their mind-power. When you come into - kingdom, you are to renew your mind, use common sense to reach your goals and cultivate your mind power. When your mind reminds you of your past, cleanse it out daily, plant a new future. Grow into greatness; don't allow yourself and others sabotage your future by reminding you of your past mistakes. **Your mind is the domain of creativity, the domain of wealth, the incubator of purpose, the place of creation.** Watch what you plant in your garden, JUNK IN, JUNK OUT.

> *Say I AM a MILLIONAIRE, stop allowing the thief of your past, and the thief of your future to steal your present moments. Have an IAMNESS MOMENT DAILY, I am no matter what the weather say, I am no matter what my heath say, I am no matter what my bank account say, I am rich, I am health, I am God's number 1 best Interest, I am a world traveler, I am that I am!*

You desire to be a doctor then think like a doctor; you desire to be a dentist, than think like a dentist; you desire to be an attorney, think like an attorney; you desire to be a millionaire then think rich, wealthy, overcoming thoughts. **Thoughts become things.** You desire to go to the NFL or NBA then develop, discipline and practice. Put the image of greatness within you! Have a burning desire to win. Surround yourself with that which you want to become. **Like attracts like.** Your present is a reflection of your future. **Dress yourself** up **for where you are going and not where you have been.** Deprogram all negative events, negative situations and program your mind for SUCCESS! Warfare is not outside of you; it's between your ears. You have got to cast down every negative thought, negative image; negative conditioning that is outside of Christ. Cast down religious error, religious tradition that does not exalt the Christ within. Jesus said 'the kingdom is within you, kingdom come! (See the chapter on KING SOLOMON)

Now see again, a fresh revelation of Genesis 1. When you see dominion over the fish of the sea, you will see a seafood franchise. When you see dominion over the air, you will see your own airplane service with jets, church owned super malls, credit unions, banks, mayors of our very own incorporated cities. Prophetically God is realigning us for kingdom domination in the Earth. Your business, your family, church, community, city, state and nation will flourish again, as you become armed and dangerous with the accurate wisdom to uproot a legacy of poverty and start a legacy of wealth establishing you as the territorial king!

Prophetic word received while writing.

You will begin to see a **shifting in power.** Those who were in authority will begin to be removed. I will establish a people unto myself, and these people shall move as a voice to the nations, liberating themselves from the bondage of the past.

You will witness a **transfer of riches** from one kingdom to another, and you will receive a fresh revelation of my glory establishing you as my **kings of the earth.** Nations shall come unto you, crooked places shall be made straight, dry places shall experience rivers in the desserts, and the **barren women shall sing again.**

I will establish a new order, shall unveil those who I have hid just for this day, new systems and governmental churches shall emerge from this anointing, and shed the old, put on the new. Many shall prosecute you; continue in the grace that I am giving. Apostolic base and headquarters shall be established officiating events that will cause a new economy to arise from the church to fulfilled my mandate in regions, in the nations and across the seas, and I will establish you again as the new power and principality of light . . .

MILLIONAIRE DAILY AFFIRMATION

I am GOD'S rich child of the rich universe. From all points of the Universe I attract wealth. I now attract all that has been mine since the foundation of the world. The father of the universe decreed over me to have dominion, supernatural infinite wisdom and divine intelligence of the Holy Spirit illuminates my mind and enlightens my millionaire path. I now find my very own royal road to riches. I experience a divine abundance of new money daily. I come into a company of angels who guide me daily in all financial affairs and I buy all things in cash. I am a magnetic symbol of wealth, I create wealth, I manufacture wealth, and I am a wealth magnet. I am coming into a wealthy place. Old cycles of poverty I command to go, new cycles of prosperity now come into my world, and it is so good. I attract the right relationships, clients, and contract daily. My income now doubles as I practice the law of seed time and harvest through tithing/offerings and abundance is my account.

Millionaire Summary

Become acquainted with wealth people, 95% of sales, business is received the first 30 seconds of interview, your dress, confidences, be an expert at your business.

- Money gives you authority in the earth
- Wealth is not gained by your income its what you do after 5 pm
- Wealth is your birthright
- Deep in your subconscious mind is a multi-million dollar idea
- Think and grow rich
- Purge your mind and environment from every poverty thinking, lack thinking, poverty stealing, negative person, idea and attitude about money

- Your desire for money must become the same desire as the creator to serve Create a service to serve 6.6 billion people, get there attention!
- Stir up the creative gifts of God and create wealth
- The woman at the well said within herself, "If I can only touch the hem of his garment then I will be made whole." (self talk)
- Find a need and fill it in your community
- Develop a consciousness of the position of wealth, influence, affluence for your future
- Bathe, soak and drench your mind with wealth, prosperity producing thoughts at bedtime
- Jesus disciple the rich and feed the poor
- Who you associate with will determine your destiny
- Marriage is a partnership, marry a mind not a behind
- Market yourself
- Increase the demands on you
- Become a self-made millionaire thru multi-level network marketing
- Live by kingdom principles
- Wake up with a wealth meditation, **SHOUT** money cometh
- Bless the rich
- Circulate with the rich develops a rich complex. Plant a money tree in your house
- Deliver yourself from every negative, demeaning. Poverty-stricken person, church, and organization
- As a man thinketh in his heart so is he
- Be ambitious
- Be willing to be mentored by experts of your chosen field of interest

The laws of MONEY

- Money chases ideals
- Money is a divine ideal of God
- Money has to be attracted to you
- Money is a medium of exchanged.

- Money has to be invested wisely
- Money escapes the hand of the unskilled
- Money is a symbol; place the symbols in your mental realm
- Money has to become your servant, not your boss
- Money has to have a reason to come to you
- Money is designed to cultivate. To the degree you allow money to flow out, the law of seedtime and harvest multiplies it over and over again
- Develop relationships with the rich

Meditation process to manifest

1. Sit comfortably, with a straight back, feet flat on the ground, (use a pillow under your feet if you are too short)
2. Focus on your breathing. Feel the breath moving in and out of your body. Do this for a few minutes, until you feel yourself relax
3. Check over your body for any areas of tension or tightness, then focus on that area and drop it, relax it, focus on your breath pouring into that area, releasing any tension
4. Slow your breathing right down, so that you are very, very relaxed
5. When you are ready, begin your meditation, examples are given later in the article
6. When you have completed the meditation, return your attention to the room or garden where you are meditating from. Notice the clothes on your skin, the chair beneath you, and your feet on the floor. Then wiggle your fingers and toes to bring you back completely.
7. Make sure you keep a journal of your meditative experiences, as sometimes things that show up in your meditations (just like dreams) will make more sense further down the track than they do now.
8. Finally you may need to do some grounding exercises if you are feeling a bit light-headed or vague. Examples of Grounding Exercises include walking around barefoot on grass, eating or drinking something, washing the dishes and stretching exercise

John D. Rockefeller (1839-1937)

After graduating from high school in 1855, he worked as a bookkeeper and clerk in Cleveland, Ohio. Amid the Allegheny oil boom of the 1860s, his dealings in commodities led naturally to refining and an operation that in 1870 emerged as Standard Oil, of which he was named president. It was at first only one of many small outfits, but under his legacy it absorbed most of its competitors, and by 1881 it controlled about 90 percent of the nations oil business, benefiting from what many considered unfair advantages, such as railroad rebates. In 1882 Standard Oil invented the trust to get around laws against owning businesses in more than one state; in 1892 the standard Oil trust was theoretically broken up as an illegal monopoly, but it survived until 1911 by the rise of another novelty, the holding company. Rockefeller retired in 1897. By 1922 he had given away about a billion dollars to family members and charity and kept only about twenty million for himself.

Cornelius Vanderbilt 1794-1877

At sixteen he bought his first sailing vessel to ferry passengers and produce between his native Staten Island and New York City; in 1829 he started a steamship line. He set his rates so low that his rivals either had to pay him to avoid their routes or had to sell out to him. During the gold rush his faster, cheaper passage from New York to San Francisco captured most of the traffic. Foreseeing American shipping's decline, he abruptly sold his fleet in the early 1860s to concentrate on Railways; he eventually got hold of the Hudson River Railroad and the New York Central and combined them and acquired the Lake Shore & Michigan Southern to establish a through route between New York and Chicago in 1873. He passed on most of his fortune to his son, William H. Vanderbilt.

CHAPTER 2

Releasing the Millionaire's Genius E-zine

This chapter will serve as a defining moment for you as a parent, teacher, pastor, business leader, Corporate CEO and millionaires in the making to turn on your's and employee's e-zine and your children's genius e-zine at an early stage; to unlock the creativity, the stuff that materialize dreams and to **increase your capacity to manifest riches, increase effectiveness and productivity.**

Millionaire Status E-zine- means unlimited force of energy with inexhaustible possibilities. No longer be stagnated by others opinions and their scotomas! You are tired of being sabotaged, mesmerized, paralyzed by your past and hypnotized by religiosity. You are tired of being broke, busted and disgusted. No longer can you tolerate small mindedness; no longer can you stay in a comfort zone of poverty. You are determined and ready to take jurisdiction of your rule by Turning on your Millionaire Genius e-zine!!!

> *Man the Apex of Creation, engineered with an innate desire, taste for beauty, extraordinary drive for excellence, uniqueness patent with the essence of greatness, genius abilities and endowed genetically designed with the DNA chromosomes of the maker of the universe. Once his divinity is lit, imagination is awaken will pioneer new epoch expand worlds thru his inexhaustible incredible mind!*
>
> *Dr. Israel Prince*

Ezine?

Ezine has been a word used to denote a small fraction of ability in relation to the whole. Marketing company's sale certain items, i.e. magazines, etc and send their distributors a small ezine of the greater product to show them a sample of the magnificent discovery.

Millionaire Status Principle #32
Release your Millionaire Genius ezine?

The Millionaire Genius -ezine is a term to describe that humans use only a small fraction of their genius power which equates to an ezine. My assignment is to make people aware so that they can release the other 99% of untapped abilities within. Millionaire ezine is the creative energy of unlimited inexhaustible divine riches genetically designed within each man.

Step into your Power!

Now you have matured to recognize its past time to come into your Millionaire status (all the universe has ordained for your life).

Divine opportunities sometimes are missed and gone because many failed to see the season of divine overflow by being stuck in an old season. You are reading this by divine providence. God has spoken a **now** word into your being. Now its time to execute, but there are blind spots, psychological waste, mental baggage and people who can't see the Magic within you!

So Genius, what does it all mean?

Genius ultimately means someone of superior being in terms of intellect.

As a society we often live in awe of brilliant achievements of others that we set ourselves apart from being geniuses. We constantly look for concrete evidence of separation, of difference, of superiority, and above all justification to understand these great minds. We look to Einstein, Mozart, Aristotle, and Shakespeare for understanding, for answers, and for clues into their worlds.

We set them apart from society and put them under a fine microscope. However related genetics are, and however large their role, our intelligence and thus our achievements as individuals are not pre-determined at birth. We are still people of creativity and imagination, which are not products of inscriptions on DNA. As Wang (2000) says, "The insights into genius will likely not be found in finer slicing, but rather, like Einstein's theories, in some more unifying model." We should not look for a simple answer to explain something as complex as the human mind.

Young Millionaire minds in jeopardy of a prehistoric system!

Mentoring the 3rd millennium Millionaire's IN THE MAKING into the arenas of business ownership verses being in commercials and being a consumer. The advantage of purposeful engagement at the junior high level is to incubate young entrepreneurs to create a new economy and stimulate the minds of teens who are not called to the fields of sports. Eighty-five percent of high school graduates do not enter college. They make up 50% of inner city youth that hang all there hopes on going to professional football or basketball leagues to escape the struggle of poverty and crime not realizing their Genius Millionaire abilities of becoming a doctor, scientist, CEO of their own corporation, music moguls, or even an affluent attorney like Johnnie Cochran.

Who is mining your child's mind?

Begin to Program your child to think outside of the traditional "get a job" mind set. Genius ability cannot be released in an environment that doesn't cultivate brilliant minds, and teach the child to discover their abilities. A Genius mind creates, discovers and analyzes. Their purpose is greater than regurgitating past knowledge to pass a test to live in the confines of a prehistoric system.

Einstein quoted, "Imagination is more important than knowledge." Bill Gates didn't receive the Microsoft ideal from a system, he created his own system from his genius ability and became the richest man in the world, according to Forbes Magazine.

Schools systems indoctrinate a child's mind over 6 hours a day, over 30 hours a week, while parents statistically spend only about 3 waking hours a day 15 hours a week engaging with their child (ren).

Most weekends are spent in leisure and in this IPOD generation where 9 year old's have cell phones and teens spend hours on the internet. The child's mind is limited in an environment that doesn't train them to become self-sufficiency, entrepreneurs, business ownership, and owning their own franchises by the age 30. The reason schools make NFL, NBA players is due to the programming of this sport in their mind at the middle school level, they practice this sport and then only 1 out of 1000 make it to the next level, when you program your child to think like a millionaire at age eight, practice millionaire principals, mediate on rich images their capacity to manage is increase, at age 30 they should not be in debt.

Millionaire Status Principle #33

Millionaires Live Outside Of Systematic Thinking! The Genius millionaire mindset has to be cultivated, wealth, prosperity, riches, the skills impressed in his/her consciousness at an early age.

The reason many athletes make it to the next level is that they become basketball, they become football, and they eat, sleep, and dream this in their mentality. This manual is designed to raise up Genius millionaires who will eat, sleep, and dream themselves into the ability to purchase stocks, mutual funds, bonds, own Franchises, be a CEO of their own creativity and by the age of 30 instead of following the yellow brick road of hoping and wishing.

Eighth Grade level is the place to birth Millionaires

Junior High School is the appropriate time to start the incubation for Teen Genius Millionaire's who I believe will trail blaze a path to a greater universal way of living placing satellites on planets, patent robots, create innovative surgery techniques and curing diseases. This is the time to begin birthing new entrepreneurs, inventors and placing in their consciousness the ideal of wealth and an understanding of how to attract money. It is documented that the average person doesn't read a complete book from cover to cover until the age of 45, so if they don't read, how can the impressions of wealth, skill, wisdom, ownership of business be deposited in their consciousness? It is recommended that Dr Israel be invited to your school, church and/or community group to begin the "Teen Genius Millionaire Summit."

AMERICAN SYSTEM OR AMERICAN NIGHTMARE!

Every year millions of parents entrust their young minds to teachers and administrators to develop and equip their child(ren) with the skills to be productive in society and to empower their dreams. In spite of the America education system, the dropout rate compared to college enrollment is higher each year. The traditional methods of learning and teaching a class of 35 students, consistently fail. Instead of teaching these students the focus has shifted to providing safety. Across the nation educational money has been spent to put medal detectors and security in the schools and not on books. School safety, modern dress codes and sports, has become more important than academic learning thereby the everyday a genius falls through the cracks as a result of the prehistoric outdated method of education. Millions of tax payer's money is spent in deprogramming the child genius's verses programming them! The result, a small percentage of students pass the basic classes, dropout rates have increased and college enrollment has not been impacted.

THE LEARNING STYLES, TEACHING STYLES MUST FIT THE INDIVIDUAL CHILD GENIUS WHICH IS SIGNIFICANT TO THE CHILD GENIUS' ABILITY

Statistically 35 % of students are leaving schools with a diploma in hand but they can't even read. 10 to 20% of American's are functionally illiterate.

System: (a prescribed set pattern to program in a person to get a result)

In earlier chapters we talked about the computer, placing software on it, the system set the boundaries and the limits of the computer user. Whatever system you attend determines the power of your rule or sets you up for failure. You cannot move any further than the system which taught you. Now is the age to break out of the systematic thinking to training your minds how to think beyond the systems of this world.

Closely investigate and examine the present environment i.e. childcare, school, business, church, learning environment, teaching styles, curriculum, sounds and the ratio of teacher to student.

I suggest you inquire about the "modus operandi" of learning. Inspect to ensure your child's genius is in a supportive, loving nurturing and creative environment, not a demeaning environment. *In today's society the question is and the quest of MITM program is to change the ratio of more individuals going to juvenile detention enroute to the prison system to higher education and shift their mind sets to manifesting their God destiny.*

The government of the US CLEARLY SHOWS US THAT CHILDREN ARE CONSIDERED A LIABILITY MORE THAN AN ASSET, the defense budget is tremendously higher than the education budget.

Defense Budget

Congress finalized the Defense Department's budget last week, giving President Bush the go-ahead to sign off on more than $***368 billion for the Pentagon*** in the next fiscal year. The appropriations package, which does not include the billions of dollars the president has requested for the Iraq supplemental, represents a $3.8 billion increase in the budget from FY2003. This is welcome news for the country's top defense contractors, who diligently re-enacted their annual battle for increased military spending this year. The defense industry's arsenal included strategic campaign contributions, a massive lobbying effort and an onslaught of glossy, inside-the-Beltway ads.

EDUCATION BUDGET? A $280 BILLION LESS BUDGET WE ARE PREPARING FOR WAR VERSES PREPARING CHILDREN TO SUCCEED IN THE US EDUCATION SYSTEM!!

Education (ED) currently administers a budget of about **$88.9 billion per year—$57.6 billion in discretionary appropriations and $31.3 billion in mandatory appropriations**—and operates programs that touch on every area and level of education. The Department's elementary and secondary programs annually serve more than 14,600 school districts and approximately 54 million students attending more than 94,000 public schools and 27,000 private schools. Department programs also provide grant, loan, and work-study assistance to more than 10 million postsecondary students.

That said, it is important to point out that education in America is primarily a State and local responsibility, and ED's budget is only a small part of both total national education spending and the overall Federal budget, as we explain in a primer on the Federal role in education.

The Natural Genius of Children

Every child is a genius. Similarly as the author use the word millionaire. It doesn't necessarily mean every person will become a millionaire, but it denotes every person has the capacity to become a millionaire given the right tools, environment, skills, and mentorship. THE POSSIBILITIES, THE POTENTIAL OF BECOMING A MILLIONAIRE, RELEASING CHILD GENETIC ACRONOMICAL POWERS ARE HIGHER WHEN HE/SHE IS PLACED IN THE LABORATORY OF DISCOVERY!

That doesn't mean that every child can paint like Picasso, compose like Mozart, act like Denzel, produce films like Spike Lee, be a strategists like Colin Powel, sing like Stevie Wonder, write scripts like Steven Spielberg or score 150 on an I.Q. test. But every child is a genius, came in the earth with the genetic code of the maker of universe, according to the original meanings of the word "genius," which are; "to give birth" (related to the word genesis) and "to be zestful or joyous," (related to the word genial). Essentially, the real meaning of genius is to "give birth to the joy" that is within each child. Every child is born with that capacity. Each child comes into life with wonder, curiosity, awe, spontaneity, vitality, flexibility, and many other characteristics of a joyous being. An infant has twice as many brain connections as an adult. The young child masters a complex symbol system (their own native language) without any formal instructions. Young children have vivid imaginations, creative minds, and sensitive personalities. These youthful traits are highly valued from an evolutionary perspective: the more species evolve, the more they carry youthful traits into adulthood (a process called "neotony" or "holding youth"). It is imperative that we, as educators and parents, help preserve these genius characteristics of children as they mature into adulthood, so those capacities can be made available to the broader culture at a time of incredible change.

Unfortunately, there are strong forces working at home, in the schools, and within the broader culture, to stifle these genius qualities in children. Many children grow up in homes which put an active damper on the qualities of genius. Factors in the home like poverty, depression and anxiety, pressure on kids to grow up too soon, and rigid ideologies based on hate and fear, actively subdue the qualities of genius in childhood such as playfulness, creativity, and wonder. Schools also put a damper on childhood genius through testing (creativity can't thrive in an atmosphere of judgment), labeling of kids as learning disabled or

ADD, boring teachers, and regimented curriculum. Finally, the broader culture, especially mass media, represses the genius in our children through its constant onslaught of violence, mediocrity, and repugnant role models.

The good news is that there is much that a teacher or parent can do to help children reawaken their natural genius. First, and most importantly, adults need to reawaken their own natural genius—find within themselves the source waters of their own creativity, vitality, playfulness, and wonder. For when children are surrounded by curious and creative adults, they have their own inner genius sparked into action. Second, adults need to provide simple activities to activate the genius of children. Something as simple as a story, a toy (Einstein said that a simple magnetic compass awakened his love of learning at the age of four), a visit to a special place, or a question, can unlock the gates to a child's love of learning. Third, create a "genial" atmosphere at home or school, where kids can learn in a climate free from criticism, comparison, and pressure to succeed. Treat each child as a unique gift from God capable of doing wonderful things in the world . Finally, understand that each child will be a genius in a totally different way from another child. Forget the standard I.Q. meaning of genius, and use models like **the theory of multiple intelligences** to help kids succeed on their own terms. By following these simple guidelines for awakening each child's natural genius, you will be contributing immeasurably to the welfare of your children and to the world they will inherit someday.

Einstein under the Microscope, Relatively Speaking

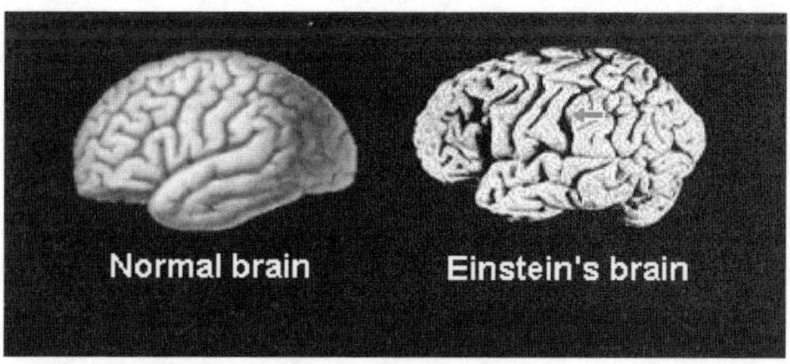

Society seems to view Einstein as if he knew some kind of secret that the rest of us didn't. Many have said that even if we knew his technique we still would not become Einstein's. Some scientific studies of Einstein's brain have been performed in an effort to prove that this statement is, in fact, true. Cardoso's 1997 editorial discusses the research that Marian Diamond, a professor from Berkley, did on Einstein's brain.

The group concluded that the greater number of glial cells 'oligodendroglia'—helper cells that speed neural communication—per neuron might indicate the neurons in Einstein's brain had an increased "metabolic need." They needed and used more energy. In this way, perhaps Einstein had better thinking abilities and conceptual skills. (Cardoso, 1997)

Cardoso's (1997) editorial goes on to discuss other findings relating to the anatomy of Einstein's brain. The Faculty of Health Sciences at McMaster University compared Einstein's brain to others and found that it was 15% wider than other brains that were studied. The researcher's noted that, "Visuospatial cognition, mathematical thought, and imagery of movement are strongly dependent on this region." The researchers thought that this may attribute to why Einstein solved problems the way that he did. Furthermore, in this same area "Einstein's brain was unique in that it did not have a groove, called a sulcus, that normally runs through" part of the area (Cardoso, 1997). Wang (2000) commented about this finding in his article, as well, saying that it was a unique feature "that may have allowed the brain's neurons to connect more effectively with each other." Despite these findings we have yet to research others to see if there is any correlation between these characteristics and brilliant minds. Wang (2000) brings up a good point in asking, " What [did] we really hope to find?" He also points out that Einstein's brain were no bigger than normal and that it was in fact smaller than average. As mentioned before, most of the research regarding genius lacks credibility. This includes these findings because they do not mean much unless others like them are discovered. Cordoso (1997) suggests that modern technology, such as magnetic resonance imaging (MRI) and positron emission tomography (PET), will enable scientists to study brain activity more accurately to arrive more firm and meaningful conclusions. Until then Einstein's "secret" and others remain elusive.

Einstein, arguably one of the most brilliant minds, does not bring us any closer to understanding his intellect or others. The majority of people do not even understand the concepts that made him famous, let alone possess the ability to dissect his thought processes, but even so psychologists continue their efforts.

Experiments on Genius or shall we say Genius Experiments

Some have even gone as far as trying to match the intellectual capabilities of geniuses to prove that with hard work one can achieve any level of intelligence. In an article published by Hulaboo (2000) Dr. Anders Ericsson, a psychologist at Florida State University, is mentioned as being one that believes that, "prodigy performance, in any field, lies within the grasp of anyone who cares to try hard enough." The article goes on to discuss studies in which prodigy skills are mastered. As Cordoso proposed in her article, some neuroscientists used positron-emission tomography (PET) to monitor the long-term working memory in action.

Dr. Tzourio-Mazoyer's team found that Mr. Gamm, their subject, was using more of his brain than normal controls, as he performed his mathematical tricks. He appeared to be using his long-term memory to store the working results that he needed to complete his calculations- for example, all the dividends and remainders of a division sum. In other respects, Mr. Gammas' brain does not appear notably unusual. Nor does he perform exceptional aptitude on tests of skills that lie outside his area of expertise, such as verbal recall. Moreover, Mr. Gamma, who is now 26, was not born with his computing ability. He developed his skills, through four hours of practicing daily, only after he had passed the ripe age of 20. (Hula boo, 2000)

Findings like these seem to go against all the claims that genius is born. The subject had chosen an area to master and put hard work into it. Not only that, but he did not start until after adulthood, which refutes the argument that people are born with these innate gifts. The article goes on to discuss how a "Hungarian doctor named Laszlo Polgar and his wife created a trio of world-class chess champions out their own daughters" (Hulaboo, 2000).

Although these experiments seem to lead to some type of finding we have yet again traveled in a circle in terms of reaching any clear conclusion. The article concludes with the argument of Ellen Winner, a psychologist from Boston College, who says that "only children with the rage to master a skill can make it through the grueling years of training needed to achieve expert ability. The rage to master may be the point at which nature unequivocally makes its constraints felt" (Hulaboo, 2000). What really sums it up is when "Dr. Ericsson concedes that there might be a genetic component separating the child willing to persevere with a rigorous schedule from the child who would rather play a videogame" (Hulaboo, 2000). So it seems as sure as they convince you of one idea they turn around and agree that genius may be genetically linked. This leads us straight into the argument that children are born geniuses.

You can't take the Genes out of Genius

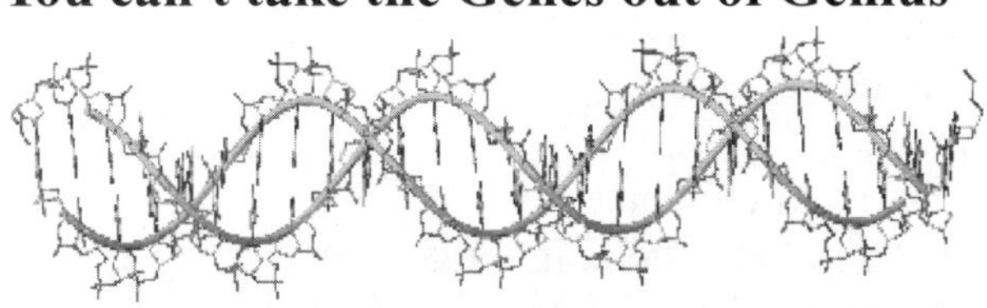

Although genius may not lie in one single gene, and to think that would be a bit childish, it seems that genes are the only thing there is a reasonable consensus among psychologists. It is more sensible to believe that genius comes from genetics in the regards that genes enable certain abilities and that, in turn, those abilities combine to enable genius. More often though the link between genes and genius is misconceived. It is not as simple as saying there is a so called "genius gene." In his book, *Genius Explained*, Howe (1999) discusses the misconceptions and the more accurate story of genetics and genius. Howe says, "In reality, rather than thinking of a gene as exerting some influence that directly affects a complex psychological characteristic, it would be more accurate to imagine the relatively immediate effect of genetic inputs being to affect, say, the production of some or other Hormone." (p.201). He goes on to say, "So even when it is indisputable that genetically based influences upon human variability have been among the contributing influences determining the rate and direction of an individual person's progress, it would be wrong to conclude that any traits or activities that have been affected by those genetic inputs have been straightforwardly determined by them." (Howe, 1999, p.201). Although Thomas Edison was once defined genius as 1% inspiration and 99% perspirations, it seems there is no denying that our genes play some role in our intellectual abilities. Steve Allen (1993) brings up the point in his article that, "We can see in the first syllable of the word a clue to its original Roman meaning, which survives in such words as gene, genetics, and genealogy."

How to Teach or Learn Anything Eight Different Ways

One of the most remarkable features of the theory of multiple intelligences is how it provides *eight different potential pathways* to learning. If a teacher is having difficulty reaching a student in the more traditional linguistic or logical ways of instruction, the theory of multiple intelligences suggests several other ways in which the material might be presented to facilitate effective learning. Whether you are a kindergarten teacher, a graduate school instructor, or an adult learner seeking better ways of pursuing self-study on any subject of interest, the same basic guidelines apply. Whatever you are teaching or learning, see how you might connect it with

- words (linguistic intelligence)
- numbers or logic (logical-mathematical intelligence)
- pictures (spatial intelligence)
- music (musical intelligence)
- self-reflection (intrapersonal intelligence)
- a physical experience (bodily-kinesthetic intelligence)
- a social experience (interpersonal intelligence), and/or
- an experience in the natural world. (naturalist intelligence)

For example, if you're teaching or learning about the law of supply and demand in economics, you might read about it (linguistic), study mathematical formulas that express it (logical-mathematical), examine a graphic chart that illustrates the principle (spatial), observe the law in the natural world (naturalist) or in the human world of commerce (interpersonal); examine the law in terms of your own body [e.g. when you supply your body with lots of food, the hunger demand goes down; when there's very little supply, your stomach's demand for food goes way up and you get hungry] (bodily-kinesthetic and intrapersonal); and/or write a song (or find an existing song) that demonstrates the law (perhaps Dylan's "Too Much of Nothing?").

You don't have to teach or learn something in all eight ways, just see what the possibilities are, and then decide which particular pathways interest you the most, or seem to be the most effective teaching or learning tools. The theory of multiple intelligences is so intriguing because it expands our horizon of available teaching/learning tools beyond the conventional linguistic and logical methods used in most schools (e.g. lecture, textbooks, writing assignments, formulas, etc.). To get started, put the topic of whatever you're interested in teaching or learning about in the center of a blank sheet of paper, and draw eight straight lines or "spokes" radiating out from this topic. Label each line with a different intelligence. Then start brainstorming ideas for teaching or learning that topic and write down ideas next to each intelligence (this is a spatial-linguistic approach of brainstorming; you might want to do this in other ways as well, using a tape-recorder, having a group brainstorming session, etc.). Have fun!

It's been reported that Einstein and Picasso were dyslexic, Edison, Neil BALDWIN, WERE CALLED INATTENTIVE, DREAMY, DISTRACTED AND DRITED off from the norm of most children, even Michael Jordan was cut from a basketball team.

Engage with the Child Genius

Many parents spend more time on the road to and from work than good positive time with their children cultivating, enhancing curiosity or stimulating creative brilliant mind of the child genius. Then once the average wage earner returns home, they have the attitude that it's TV time and many spend hours watching their favorite sitcom(s) with little or no true positive engagement with their children. Girls 18 grow up without knowing how to cook an egg while boys learn how to make cat calls at girls. Mentoring is the missing link! A child must be taught how to think and not primarily react. Many inner city children are what you call Latch-key children, children exposed to negative scenes, negative images, drug and alcohol is introduced to them and parents wonder why they deviate to crime. The boys and girls clubs are the parents for many children though these centers offer awesome fun they don't often provide the tools to release the child's greatness!

There's a CRY FOR Mother's like HANNAH'S?

There is a call for mothers like Hannah who will release their children to the Temple to the priests. fathers like Jacob who will speak, for me and my house we will serve the lord and mothers who will lock into the vision of their husband cultivating, praying and igniting the child genius's destiny! Mother's who will complete their soul mate's assignment and not compete, marriage is a partnership , society is losing children due to the temptation of moving women form the greatest role of being a mom, woman should be in corporate America, but lead your children to the altar. A young girl has to be groomed into a princess, groomed into a Queen, like wise a young man has to be groomed into a prince, process into a King.

Statical Analysis of American Systems

Basic education is about turning on the light of truth! The public school system cannot keep our children attention in the seat, dropout rate since 1980 has been 30%. Only 16% of America's students graduate competent in math according to the **National Assessment Governing Board. Education** is supposed to be the proper cultivation of the gifts, talents of the individual, releasing their abilities through the acquisition of knowledge.

The self knowledge of their history, whether Europeans, African, or Native American, the current study of American History is nothing more than the indoctrination of the Americans specifically white male superiority which limits the reach of other minorities, women in society to have equal assess to the same opportunities, Sociologist's describes it as a 'Strain Theory", it a strain once a minority realized he/she is out of school, hopes to climb the corporate ladder becomes a strain.

Belief system regulates what you will accomplish in life!

You are a product of your environment, your child environment has to have the tools to take them to the next level, as we have discussed a child is 75% of his /her day is not in the home, it's in a learning environment, this will determine whether they become a child millionaire or a statistical in juvenile court.

If a child is never taught about his/her true history, it will limit the reach of accomplishments of their life; the first principal in life is to know thyself!

A Eurocentric history perspective is quite hostile to black students, they are not seen an important. How can a person become an International business leader when in their early childhood reading and high school, church environment they only become familiar with Eurocentric history, this is why you witness black on black drive by shooting, young black males don't see any important blacks besides Martin Luther King, for me to come into all that the father has ordained for my life , I need a education of my true culture roots, obvious you as a reader know that the as African, your destiny started out as Kings and Queens not on a slave ship to America to be chained up! Red, yellow, black or white all are precious in his sight!

The mind is a terrible thing to waste, it has to be enlightened to truth, illuminated to understand their true greatness, if a child doesn't know his history, as Marcus Garvey said, it's like a tree disconnected from the root but its being wasted each day a child who has millionaire genes is exposed to materials he can't used, or not stimulated in his area of greatness, school teacher told Edison parents he was retarded, yet today our lives of lit by the glory of his thoughts!

Greatness is discovered, true teachers have to see the angel in the rock.

Auditory, Visual or Kinesthetic Learning Styles?

Tapping into genius ability begin by observing their learning style. Every child has a different learning style, according to their culture they learn different, new system must accommodate these variety of learning styles. New education system are now being set in place, not to deposit into the child genius, but to draw out of the child, his God given gift to the world, training him/her to discovery life from within, instead of basing their future whether they pass the WASL or State test, most gifted children get bored within the public system, due their mind power is not stimulated.

Among black urban youth, two pioneer post-civil rights entrepreneurs stand out: film maker Spike Lee and music executive Russell Simmons. Both in their early 40s, Lee and Simmons are the forerunners of this new breed of urban entrepreneurs. As Chief Executive Officer of Rush Communications, Simmons leads the second largest black-owned entertainment company in the U.S. (Black Entertainment Television Holding, Inc., is first.) Since founding Def Jam Recordings in 1985 – the largest subsidiary of Rush communications – Simmons has methodically spread his reach across the entertainment industry into fashion, film, television, publishing and advertising. Most recently, he has launched an Internet venture. A corporate executive and not an artist, he is considered the consummate example of a true player in the hip-hop music and entertainment industry.

Likewise, Spike Lee is another important purveyor of hip-hop culture who has methodically reinvented himself from an artist/producer of films, commercials, books and clothing for his production company, 40 Acres and a Mule, Inc. to President and Creative Director of Spike DDB Needham Worldwide, a leading Madison Avenue advertising agency. In an unusual joint venture where Lee owns 51 percent of the company, he hopes to employ his entrepreneurial aptitude and insights into urban America. As DDB Needham begins to shift its vision in advertising from mass markets to targeted consumer cohorts with tailored messages, Spike DDB is poised to become a leader in urban advertising.

Because of Simmons and Lee, the business development ethos of hip-hop culture is alive and well among the current generation of artists and executives.

For example, Bad Boy Entertainment CEO, Sean "Puffy" Combs, is proprietor of a restaurant, has established himself in the fashion industry with a signature clothing line for men, publishes a hip-hop magazine, and has most recently launched an Internet venture. Other examples of Hip-Hop entrepreneurship include the Wu-Tang Clan's apparel line and clothing store; Fat Joe's barbershop; and DJ Spinderella's She Thing Salon/Day Spa in Queens, New York. Although many of these entrepreneurial ventures have been successful, huge challenges often face those artists who have little or no business experience.

Team synergy!

You cannot reach certain plateau's without streamlining deleting irrelevant materials, mental blocks, low energy entities from your life, your business will only produce at the level of capacity of the companies Team synergy and the consciousness of the mastermind strategists!

Jesus Christ The C.e.o. Of The Universe Recruited 12 Millionaires To Founded His World Global International Vision! They Locked Into His Vision, He Had Only One Agenda! One Sound Was Echoed Which Originated From The Master!

Do you see the young woman or the old woman? (for MIMP Training purpose)

A famous perceptual **illusion** in which the brain switches between seeing a young girl and an old woman (or "wife" and "mother in law")

Scotomas are blind spots individuals build up through a belief system that was created by self and others. These illusions brought by negative programming prevents one's perception from moving to a higher level thereby interfering with the business growth, relationships, marriages and cash flow. Once blind spots are identified individuals, companies, churches and corporations can function at the optimum level of growth and come into the MILLIONAIRE STATUS!

Millionaire Summary

MOST MILLIONAIRES ARE SELF MADE WITH THE GENIUS ABILITY ENGINEERED BY THE CREATOR OF THE UNIVERSE AND THIS POWER HAS TO BE STIMULATED AND TURN ON! ENGAGE WITH YOUR CHILD INSTEAD OF DISENGAGE.

James G Fair 1831-1894

This Irish immigrant failed to strike it rich mining in California and Nevada, so he set up a lumber business to serve prospectors on the Comstock Lode. In the 1870s he and a group of associates got control of a property near Virginia City, Nevada and in 1873 the resulting Consolidated Virginia Mine produced enough silver to potentially destabilize the U.S. money supply. Fair converted his share of the wealth into railroads, buildings, land, and high living. He served a six-year Senate term but was better known for his family's sad decline; Divorced, alienated from his children, he died alone. He stipulated in his will that anyone able to prove themselves to be his widow or child would be entitled to fifty dollars.

REFERENCES AND FURTHER READING

Citations from parallel literature quoted in the commentaries are taken from the following sources.

The Everyday Genius . . . . Peter Kline 1988

The Fire Within . . . . James Giles 2001

Mentored by a Millionaire . . . . Steven Scott

Three Magic Words . . . . US Andersen 1989

Profiles of a Genius . . . . Gene Landrum

Money Magnetism . . . . J. Donald Walters

Secrets of a Millionaire Mind . . . . T. Harv Eker

The New Color of Success . . . . Niki Mitchell

The Riches Man Whoever Lived. . . . . Steven Scott

Millionaire Profiles

"Unlocking the Divine"

Any philosophy that support that the Creative Intelligence of the universe would create man in bondage and leave him bound would be to dishonor the Creative Powers which we call God!

Inside of every man you meet is a divine spark of divinity at a different level and stage that needs to be lit, each day salute the divinity within each man you meet in reality they are you in a unconscious state.

Water rises to its proper level. The condition of your consciousness will determine the level of abundance, level of prosperity and riches in your life. Your mentality reflects your present reality. Your belief system is the thermostat of gauging what you will accomplish in life. What level of mindset do you have? Locate where you are, then locate what level of prosperity, tangible income you desire to enjoy. You will never acquire wealth with a religious mindset, money chases creative ideas. Execute your game plan to accomplish the dream.

God has no problem with the amount of zero's on your check, whether it's 5 or 6 digit monthly income is solely up to you, according to your faith be it unto you. The only limitation you have is the one you set or allow others to set for you.

Millionaire Status Principle #34

If you can conceive it, you can ACHIEVE IT!

When you see other's living in fancy million dollar estates, riding in the newest BMW's, May Bach or Royal Bentley, eating at the finest restaurants, dining in elegance or sporting the hottest fashions from Paris, how do you react? Do you bless the rich, or do you say, who does she/he think they are? Resentment, envy and bitterness will block 85% of the prosperity that will come in your direction. These thoughts in your consciousness prevent wealth from being created!

If you curse the rich, rich you will never be. If you bless the rich then you will become rich, wealthy and affluent with influence. Money escapes the minds and the hands of the unkind, and unskilled.

Is there a certain personality, certain genetic trait or simply an innate **hunger for life**? Certain ingredients are essential to become a millionaire. Millionaires are born in all walks of life and matriculate from all communities like Famous Amos, Walt Disney and Howard Hughes.

You can't place a large dream in a small minded person.

Synergy (The interaction of two or more agents or forces so that their combined effect is greater than the sum of their individual effects) is one of many characteristics that must be developed in becoming a multi-millionaire in society. When you study modern day successful and highly famous individuals, despite their past, became Champions in a variety of arena's like, Leonardo da Vinci, Henry Ford, Albert Einstein and Nelson Mandela. There are no two fingerprints. Stevie Wonder, Steven Spielberg, Oprah Winfrey, Elvis Presley, Bill Gates, Maya Angelo and Martin Luther King release a higher purpose to serve the earth. Find your ***Gethsemane and stay there as Job said, "Until my change come."***

Millionaire status is not just about the Benjamin's, the tangibles of life, it's about the fighter within, and the desire to release your gift to the world, in spite of difficulty, knowing that out of the tomb of hopelessness came the master of the universe. When the odds are against you, then this is your greatest moments.

True riches within your grasp cannot always be measured in money. Put this philosophy of millionaire status in consciousness: Have a resolve today, don't allow problems to paralyze you, sabotage your destiny or destroy relationships. Allow your set backs to become set up's for future Miracles. Take a break in life, but swing back. Smile big, laugh, pray long, give generously, forgive quickly, love deeply, hold a child often, and live on the sunny side of the mountain.

Millionaire Status Principle #35

Acquaint thyself with the Rich!

Most millionaires have the ability to bounce back from adversity.

Colonel Sanders - at the age of 40, made chicken for people who passed by his service station in Corbin, Kentucky. He didn't have a restaurant then and served the diners in his home on his own dining room table. Sanders was forced to sell his property to make way for Interstate 75. He lived off his social security and based his entire career on his ability to cook. He traveled the country by car from restaurant to restaurant, eventually opening the first franchise of "Finger-lickin" good in 1952 in Salt Lake City Utah.

Edison is credited with being one of America's most persistent scientists. It's reported that he conducted thousands of experiments before he invented the electric light bulb.

Never accept defeat!!

Mary Kay Ash - Nursed her ill father from the age seven, functioned as adult while still a child. When she was 27 her first husband left her with three children under the age of eight. Her second husband died thirty days prior to the launch of Mary Kay Cosmetics.

Liz Claiborne - Nazis invaded Belgium when she was ten causing her family to flee to the United States.

Jane Fonda - Mother committed to a sanitarium with three nervous breakdowns when Jane was eleven and her mother committed suicide when she turned 12; Fonda struggled with bulimia for 23 years.

Estee Lauder- Sister has polio as a child.

Madonna- Mother died of cancer when Madonna was 5. Her everything father betrayed her by marrying the babysitter, who became the wicked stepmother.

Oprah Winfrey- One of the most influential women in America today. Not only is she a television superstar, with her talk show going into its 20th year, but she is the CEO of Harpo Studios which has produced several television movies. She is the creator of O Magazine which is an overwhelming media success. She was referred to as an illegitimate child, moved five times during her teen years. Raped at age nine molested by three family members, pregnant at fourteen and had child die at birth. A jilted relationship in Baltimore drove her to attempt suicide.

Bill Gates- The intensity and drive of Gates is legend and contagious according to Scott Oki, a senior vice president at Microsoft. He says the Gates influence is pervasive, 'We have a maniac work ethnic here, and everyone has a sense of participating in a crusade! Another says, he is consumed with winning, and uses force of will to overwhelm his adversaries.

Ted Turner- Mr. Risk Taker, college textbooks define entrepreneurship as synonymous with risk taking. Ted Turner epitomizes the consummate risk-taker in business. In 1970 he risked $100 million organization to create CNN, the rest is history.

Walt Disney- founded the Disney Brother's Studio's in Hollywood at age 22 on October 16, 1923, with a $500 loan from his Uncle Robert and a $285 loan from Brother Roy. With an advance of 2000.00 from Margaret Winkler, he produced the first successful cartoon *TROLLEY TROUBLE. Disney drew his plans for Mickey Mouse amusement park in 1948, bank debt would not permit implementation. Roy called it a fairground and accused his brother of schizoid behavior. Walt ignored his brother, borrowed $100,000 on his insurance policy, sold his Palm Springs home to help finance start–up that Roy refused to support.*

Personalities:

1. All were self starters and prodigiously productive.
2. They did not get ulcers, they gave them.
3. Most had few friends but many disciples.
4. Most did not follow the establish order, they created new paths.
5. Their persona instilled fear in associates and family (people sense a ticking time bomb ready to blow at the least provocation)
6. They reached the top but never remembered or enjoyed the journey.
7. They had childlike imagination and lived life as a fantasy.
8. Most operated on the right side of the brain, seemed abnormal, but was quite the genius.
9. Most made more friends than enemies.
10. Most were not religious, they were World servers. (Find a product that can serve the needs of the 400 billion people on the planet)

Certain attributes that were in George ***Washington Carver*** are in all us that would depict many as geniuses. In reality they found something they loved to do and they sacrificed and were **RISK** Takers. Think of ***Frank Wright***, the greatest architect in history, ***Pablo Picasso***, greatest artist of the twentieth century, and ***Michael Jordan***, greatest basketball player of the 21st century. These people defied the odds, refused to quit, and refused to bow to others when they were told it couldn't be done. **They thirst, hungered for the better life!**

When faced by a mountain, I will not quit, I will continue to climb, or I will stay there. Make a tunnel through it, or simply sit on it and turn it to a gold mine!

In order to attract wealth into your life, your subconscious mind must be opened to the ideal of wealth flowing toward you. You have to trick your mind. Your subconsciousness is the server, and the master key of all creation is your consciousness. If you can dream it, you can achieve it, but dream big, the universe cannot fill small orders! Ask for the moon, even if you land on a star!

Einstein said, "Imagination is Creation." Consciousness creates everything! Proverbs states "as a man thinketh in his heart so is he." Become consciousness of what you want. Develop a Millionaire consciousness or a Billionaire consciousness. You cannot attract wealth with a good-will, poverty consciousness and religious "some day soon" mentality. You have to destroy the slave wage mentality. Dress your mind up to where you are going not where you been!

Play music in your environment fit for Kings; get the right vibrations in your atmosphere; create the mood for creativity, play Beethoven symphony and feel the positive experience.

Locate thyself, what's holding you back from getting that college degree, becoming a business owner, writing your first book and traveling to an exotic island with your love one. Who is pulling your heart string away from God's ordained plan for your life? If it's baking cakes, cooking chicken, making the best clothes, or singing, then refine thyself, define thyself, don't allow other people opinions of you define you. Remember Colonel Sander's knock on 999 doors until he finally received one yes and today, Kentucky Fried Chicken Franchise's are International and all over the US. Remember it all began with a 65-year-old gentleman who used his $105 Social Security check to start a business.

Your optimist attitude must break forth from the pessimist crowd who will smother and kill your dream.

Get up NOW and soar as the eagles without boundaries, **find the thing you love to do,** and do it well then at your doorstep will be riches! I'm warning you to never give in to defeat, never give up on your dream, never accept failure and don't be a clone to someone else's pains and loneliness. You owe it to your self to be happy, fulfilled, and you deserve the best in life. Realize losses are upside down crosses which turn into triumphs of tomorrow! Never rehearse your past, bury it in the sands of yesterday, and dig new wells of prosperity today!

Millionaire in Greek means, abundantly supplied, without having lack, and the ability to become self reliant is the heart of every living being in the earth. Everyone came to earth with a million dollar idea inside of them, with a God changing idea locked between the corridors of their consciousness.

There are white millionaires, Hispanic millionaires, African millionaires, millionaires of all races, and the astronomical power of purpose lives within a man, not outside of him/her. God never went outside himself for anything. The creator of the universe placed in you the power to manifest wealth. You will see self made millionaires daily. One thing that we all have in common and most millionaires agree that ***there are opportunities everywhere and*** what some call junk, become other's wealth producing ideals.

Rich people and poor people have different mind sets and different energy. They radiate, and vibrate at a different level. They think, react and dream different! Many can see the angel in the rock, many can see the diamonds in coals, many can hear the masterpiece in the song, and others don't even listen. You have to learn how to turn a silver moment into a golden opportunity.

It's never too late to start, start now, instead of waiting for your laid off slip. Go in and fire yourself to the NEXT LEVEL OF LIVING, where you are the author, conductor, and the finisher of your destiny. Grasp the mindset of a millionaire, let go of your yesterday tears and move into your millionaire status years.

Celebrated African Millionaire's

Kenneth Chenault has been the CEO of American Express, a $25.9 billion financial and travel services giant since 2001. A Harvard Graduate, Forbes Magazine reported his annual income for 2004 to be in excess of $11 million. He is in the process of transforming AmEx into places where cardholders can also buy everything from financial plans to mutual funds.

W. Clement with only $100.00 and the desire to succeed he employed the principles in Think and Grow Rich and was able to build an organization that now produces a gross annual income of over thirty-six million Dollars.

Madame C.J. Walker (1867-1918)

Madame C. J. Walker grew up in poverty, unable to read or write, surviving one hardship after another. She was born in 1867 in Louisiana; she went from being a wash woman to being the first woman self-made millionaire by experimenting with various mineral and animal oils to find a remedy for her hair that was falling out. She constructed a Plant in Pittsburgh, where she founded the Leila College of Beauty and started the Walker Enterprise where she provided employment for some 3000 employees in 1905.

Arthur G. Gaston (1892-1996)

Born July 4, 1892, grew up in Demopolis, Alabama; Gaston's personal dream was to empower African Americans socially and economically. He and his wife pioneered the Booker T. Washington Business College. Gaston, during the heat of the Civil rights movement, started the Citizens Federal Saving Bank Association; by 1961 its assets exceeded $5 million. Founded the A. G. Boys Club, his bank became the largest in Alabama.

John H. Johnson (1918-2006) First African American to own and operate a major publishing company, Ebony and Jet magazines. The company has more than 3000 thousand employees and sales annually over $350 million. Johnson used his mother furniture as a security for a $500.00 loan, sent out 20,000 copies of a letter offering charter subscriptions to his new magazine and 3000 people sent in $2, annually giving him $6000.00 to start his dream!

Quincy D. Jones B. (1933) One of the highly acclaimed celebrated artists in the world, Quincy Jones began playing music at an early age, active in high school band and music, wrote first composition in high school "From the four Winds". Moved to Seattle Washington, toured the clubs and experienced the music of great musicians such as Dizzy Gillespie, Charlie Parker and Duke Ellington. Quincy won scholarships to study music at the University of Washington, Schillinger's house, and Boston Institution. He produced recordings by Michael Jackson, Tevin Campbell, Keith Washington, the Winans and many more.

Earvin 'Magic Johnson" An NBA Hall of Famer, Johnson is now a superstar in business. His corporation consists mostly of inner city businesses such as movie theaters, restaurants, shopping malls, and athletic clubs. In over ten years his corporation has grown into a $500 million empire.

Robert Johnson began Black Entertainment Television BET, in 1980, grew it and sold the television enterprise to Viacom for nearly $3 billion, making him the first black man with an estimate net worth exceeding a billion dollars.

Earl Graves begin Black Enterprise Magazine in 1970 with the focus of building wealth for generations of African Americans. He runs the magazine today with his wife and three sons boasting sales over $50 million and expanding into several other markets.

John Thompson after spending years with IBM became the top man at once of top companies in Silicon Valley. Symantec is a $1 billion company with over 14,000 employees worldwide. It is the leader in security software and has operations in over 40 countries.

> *Most of these Millionaire profiles above all agree that getting rich is not about the money. You must become service oriented, accentuate the positive in life, think different than the crowd, quit doing what you don't like, do what you love, find the real you, live in the moment, cultivate true relationships, and most of all be a giver. 85 % of millionaires are humanitarians; they give beyond the law of tithes. Find ten people and make their dream come alive!*

THE UNITED STATES OF AMERICA
FEDERAL RESERVE NOTE
ONE HUNDRED DOLLARS
THIS NOTE IS LEGAL TENDER FOR ALL DEBTS, PUBLIC AND PRIVATE
WASHINGTON, D.C.
G 05555555 A
100

CHAPTER 3

Money Magnetism

Activating The Millionaire's Personal Magnetism

Albert Einstein quoted, "Imagination is creation, and your thoughts are the preview of your Coming attraction!

So far we have discussed basic principles of magnetizing wealth, now we offer a few practical suggestions which you as a student of Truth will need to develop a daily habit of mediation to demonstrate and manifest at a higher level. You will become what you think about; you will manifest from your personal mind broadcasting system; your consciousness, and your MINDPOWER is the incubator of divine purpose! Your new money will manifest at the level of a millionaire or even a billionaire, according to the habitual daily thought energy applied in consciousness. Most people continue to manifest the same substance because they continue to focus on what they have in hand.

What exactly do you desire to manifest? How much new money do you de-

sire to manifest per day, per week, per hour, per year? The need for Concentration is paramount to the ability to manifest, whether you desire a new you, new consultants, new clients, new car, new house, new clothes, new relationship and better relationship with children. Paramahansa Yogananda says, "The greater the will, the greater the flow of energy." Will is desire plus energy, directed toward fulfillment.

Millionaire Status Principle #34

You have to practice the presence of God, thru deliberate daily quiet meditation and move in the realm of the spirit staying in a single state of concentration for hours.

Ninety-nine percent of people on the planet are manifesting at a low level because they have no medicine called meditation in their soul! I wish above all that you may prosper and be in health, even as thy soul prospers! SOUL PROSPERITY IS THRU MEDITATION! GET OUT OF THE STATE OF LACK; GET OUT OF THE STATE OF NEED, GET INTO THE STATE OF ABUNDANCE, THERE IS PLENTY UNLIMITED SUPPLY IN THE UNIVERSE!

In this Money Magnet chapter, I have enclosed the dimensions of money. This came about when I was teaching and I asked the students what they desire to manifest? Many talked about money. I ask "Who is on the 1 dollar bill; the 5 dollar bill and the 10.00 bill? How about the 50.00, 100.00, 500.00, and 1000.00 bill? Who is on the 10,000 dollar bill? Most of the people didn't know and some guessed. Well how can you manifest a thing if the mind doesn't have the correct IMPRINT, the correct image, the picture perfect of desire? The Universe is user friendly; it will give you what you give it! I suggest you meditate, then radiate, and vibrate new money by focusing on exact images. To get rid of debt , write a check out to all your creditor, don't send it, just write out the exact amount owed, and then see it paid in full on check, then rejoice, feel it, taste it, breath

it, see it and become free. If it's a better body, then use the same process, consciousness is everything! Place the new dress out, the exact figure you desire in consciousness, in mind, in mentality, then it will manifest in time. See your business explode in sales, activate your consciousness with new clients, see your master mind team of consultants, leaders grow, see your children make new grades in school, focus on the good in your spouse, accentuate the perfect in them and don't focus on what you don't want.

Declare I am a Money Magnet; I attract new money from all points of the universe. My sales increase daily, my money makes money, I tithe 10% to myself first and 10% to my storehouse. I am a money magnet; my mind is now filled with wealth producing, wealth making ideals. Money chase my ideals, my money angels now send new money in my life!

1. Develop magnetic power by thinking and acting that you are more magnetic.

2. Develop a winning personality will increase your personal magnetism.
3. Develop a likeable spirit.
4. Develop the power of concentration on a specific desired result through deliberate visualization, see it, taste it, feel it, become it!

5. Become a Money magnet by daily counting the total sum of money your desire to attract, have a definite aim!
6. Develop magnetic energy by making every person you meet feel like a King!

CHAPTER 4

Millionaire's Mindset in the Making
Basic in Investing

The Human Brain

Recently, atomic power scientists have figured that all the atoms in the human body would produce 11,400,000 kilowatts of power per hour if they could harness the astronomical energy. Based on this computation, a man or woman weighing 150 pounds is worth $85, 500,000,000. Do you know how powerful your mind is? One human brain, if unraveled, would take the entire state of Texas to stretch it to capacity. Your brain carry's electromagnetic power where it could, literally, in one year supply enough energy to light up a country the size of Iraq.

The word Genesis derives from the word Genius, root word Gene. You have the Genetic composition creative ability of the God that created the Universe. This genius power is inside of you!

Experts *say you cannot become rich in your pockets, until you become rich in your mind. Psychologists tell us we can have anything that we can mentally accept!*

Millionaire Status Principle #36

Universally there is unlimited power, ability and creativity between your ears to manifest by pushing the key called DESIRE into your meditative state.

You can produce anything! Create a Rich Image within; begin today to awake the Creative genius within you! Whenever you desire a thing, go within or go without!

The Atomic Power of creativity is within every man.

Your brain contains approximately forty eighty ounces of tissue containing one trillion brain cells, neurons, axons and dendrites. The neuron, the basic unit of the brain is a complex information processing system. Each of you're approximately one hundred billion neurons can process up to fifty thousand messages per second. Millions of messages are processed in the brain, first neurons receives the messages, process it inside the cell body, then the long fibers called dendrites, sends the message to other neurons. The messages are transmitted chemically across small gaps called synapses. Synapses are like a bridge between neurons. It is a very smart bridge because the synapses determine whether a message gets transmitted. Synapses are also important because they are where learning and memory occur. The Brain can be divided into five interconnected areas, brainstem, diencephalons, limbic, neocortex and the Spinal cord; all incoming sensory information first enters the CNS at the level of the spinal cord or brainstem. This means that the first place where patterns of activation are, are matched against previous stored areas.

The brain is comprised of two major types of specialized cells, neurons and glial cells. Inside each of these 100 billion neurons and 1 trillion glial cells is the exact same genetic material, the same genes (that's why many people say, "The fruit does not fall far from the tree"). If parent's DNA is from a rich, intelligent, purpose driven, structured, prosperity environment that produces little Einstein's, Beethoven's, and Plato's, then the child will highly produce the same effects in his or her life (given they don't alter their genes by using drugs or alcohol). Synapses are the neurotransmitters that are stored in the vesicles, which will fuse with the pre-synaptic neuron's membrane. It's important to examine the parents DNA that is a deciding factor of the child's DNA. Scientists have begin to clone humans species by splicing gene pools, this is why many celebrities are looking into artificial inseminations to keep a high probability of the same matter in their children as genius's.

Parents have the ability to increase the mental capacity of their children before birth. It's not what the mother eats, it's what they are feeding the child mental messages

Millionaire Master Key!

The Conscious Mind is the MASTER KEY, the subconscious mind is the servant, whatever you program in, it will release. You have to become conscious of what you desire to create, the universe is user friendly it will manifest upon desire!

Did you know that when you see a typical iceberg and remark how huge it is we are only seeing just a tip of the iceberg?

Well, generally 90% of an iceberg is actually below the water. In reality 30% o f the people on the planet, 6.6 billion people are taking care of the other 70%. Most people use only 5 % of their mind power and the other 95% is under water. Roughly 10% of our thought-processing occurs within the conscious part of our mind and the other 90% or so of our thoughts and decisions take place in our subconscious.

The human mind is truly unlimited in its capacities and abilities. The human mind is capable of conceiving virtually anything it is capable of conceiving. Take every computer on the planet including the gargantuan Cray or IBM supercomputer, with all of their computing and memory capacity space still represents less memory of a single human mind!

Neuroscientists tell us there are 100 billion computing cells within the human mind. The brain is so magnificent. The study of Einstein's brain revealed he only used 10% of his brain capacity yet mastered the laws of gravity, theory of relativity, spitting atoms, molecular and physics. The brain and its constituent's parts are the most complex system in the known universe, and the most unused machinery that the creator has given man to create worlds.

Power within

Tap into the unused inexhaustible powers between your ears!" What lies ahead of us, and what lies behind us, pales in significance to what lies within us!

How many Millionaires in America?

One million new U.S. MILLIONAIRES, just in 2000 alone, brought a total to 6, 850, 000 millionaires that was 2740 new millionaire's per day. Can you conceive that? Lottery millionaires, plus lawsuits, athletes and entertainment millionaires are only 1% of all US Millionaire's with 80 % have little or no college education. 85% become millionaires by doing what they love to do and fulfilling their passions! America has 271 of the world's 563 known billionaire's. You are living in the richest land in the richest era of the history of Man.

> *"The HUMAN BRAIN cannot function without set, defined goals; the mind must have a definite aim."*
>
> *Whatever is imprinted, impressed on the SUBCONSCIOUS MIND, is expressed, manifested as form in your experience.*
>
> Joseph Murphy

There is nothing divine about living a meager life, barely surviving and scratching at the bottom of the barrel. God never intended you to live form paycheck to paycheck. He placed a Million dollar ideal inside of you! There is a law of expansion where you must grow into your greatness!

Intrinsic Traits of a Millionaire's Mind

In order to produce a millionaire mindset, it's imperative to understand the purpose of your mind, the power that lives between your ears.

Being a principal in the education system, I observed that 99% children have not being taught the basic functions of the brain or how to think. The American system teaches children's to get a diploma and then get a job. (See below basic in INVESTING)

They are being systemically programmed to work at MacDonald's, and not given the skills or desire from grade 1 to own MacDonald's Franchises. That is why it's important to conduct the Millionaire in The Making Training sessions monthly to deposit and impart a millionaire entrepreneurial mindset in children starting at 8 years old.

Millionaires Are Great Executors

They don't sit around getting a small opinion concerning their world global vision with petty minded individuals. Traits of a millionaire mindset normally have a definite purpose, a definite aim and they know exactly what they want in life. They have written goals of when they desire it, and how much wealth they deserve. Many would call them arrogant, but it's really that the Millionaire's mind has a low tolerance for ignorance.

You have to learn how to walk with a genius. A millionaire would have an Einstein moment when a laser beam thought of changing the world pass thru their consciousness and the whole world has to stop, the flag come down, the traffic is jammed until this moment passes. 99% were called crazy; some were thought to be lazy since they couldn't fit into the institutional slavery system and wait on social security. They are never underachievers, mostly over achievers, they seldom underestimate their abilities, many would call them spend thrift, but in reality money is simply a means to accomplish dreams, they are not attached to it. They will risk it all, when destiny calls.

Internal Guiding System

Millionaires, those with genius abilities, have an internal guiding system that continues to operate even under pressure. Though winds, storms, may continue to hit their target, and others around them give up their dreams or call it quits, they persevere to higher levels.

A torpedo is a self-propelled projectile launched above water or below the water surface; they can be launched from a variety of air crafts, submarines and is designed to detonate on contact of target. It is programmed before launching, calibrated to hit exact placements of target even thru a crisis.

Crisis is often the "mother of innovation." To launch Apple Computers, Steven Jobs went out and begged for money for an unknown concept. He sold the first twenty-five units of Apple 1 to the Byte Shop in Mountain View and didn't know if they would work. He used his family's two bedrooms and garage as the manufacturing facility. He called vendors and pleaded for credit. These are the sacrifices of an entrepreneur, which places demands on their relationships. An entrepreneur is the first calling as a millionaire. The entree, the pioneering of a dream!

Apple made more millionaires than IBM, HP, and Digital equipment Corporation put together. These visionaries took inordinate risks, which is essence of the innovative process. Steve Jobs was a pioneer, lead the industry of the personal computer revolution.

Millionaire Status Principle #37

Millionaire family must go the distance.

A Millionaire's family, entrepreneurs spouses, children, all those connected have to give way from the normality's of life, receive their universal callings to pioneering their Global destiny! Thru coordination of knowledge and effort, in the spirit of harmony, two people, a group of master mind strategies, a business, can manifest dreams when they *agree in definite purpose , and become single minded!*

Thomas J. Stanley, Ph.D., recently published a book titled, *The MILLIONAIRE MIND*. Below I have excerpted a few key elements from the *Millionaire Mind* that will help you see what's necessary to become a Millionaire.

Basic Information:

- All were first generation, seasoned business owners, executives or professionals.
- They didn't follow the crowd.
- Most saw opportunities that others ignored.

Demographic Overview:

- 54 years of old
- On average have 3 children
- Only 2 % inherited all or part of net worth
- Small outstanding home mortgages
- 32 % business owners
- 16 % are senior corporate executives
- 10% attorneys
- Business owners are richest of the group

- 90% ARE COLLEGE GRADUATES, 52 % HAVE ADVANCED DEGREES

MILLIONAIRE'S MIND

- Have fine homes but little or no debt
- Became rich without compromising their integrity
- Spend lot of time socializing
- Focus energy to maximize the return on effort
- Spend time planning investment and often consult tax advisors
- 45 % family relocations, family counsel, 35% divorce

Millionaire's Market is the World

With the faces of American's majority ethnic groups changing in the 3rd Millennium, its imperative that Corporations, churches, business leaders keep abreast to the times. Management faces must also change to meet the demands of a changing America. Managers must seize and target the New Majority in American society. Business modalities must be user friendly by all races; by 2010 the majority race in the USA will be minorities who have other languages, needs, cultural differences that must be embraced to market the products. The businesses you have now begin moving it to a Global level. Get ready for the Hispanic American Millionaires, new faces moving into the work forces, into Network marketing companies, into all sectors of society. God said reach the WORLD, over 6.6 billion people on the planet need your services, use the superhighway internet, use the satellite radio, use the new technology to reach other nations and learn their language.

Find a need and fill it, find a hurt and heal it!

Get ready for the Hispanic Millionaires in training! Reach this new Market with your million dollar idea!

Core Values and Common Traits in the Heterogeneous Hispanic American Market

June, 2005, By Alex Camacho

"We become not a melting pot but a beautiful mosaic. Different people, different beliefs, different yearnings, different hopes, different dreams."

—Jimmy Carter

We have all heard the news: the Hispanic population in the U.S. is exploding, jumping from 22.4 million people in 1990 to nearly 40 million in 2003. And most marketers want to get to know them better, since their purchasing power is expected to grow to as much as $1 trillion by 2010. And by now, market researchers have realized that the term "Hispanic" is really just a convenient way of describing a large, heterogeneous group of people rich in diversity and cultural subtleties; a group for which a one-size-fits-all approach to marketing does not fit. Yet, the contemporary Hispanic American market shares many core values and traits that have implications for Hispanic research and Hispanic marketing.

Core Values in the Heterogeneous Hispanic Culture

Hispanics are a diverse group of people, coming to the U.S. from more than twenty different countries (in addition to the original U.S. Hispanics from the fourteenth century), with hopes of improved economic conditions, better educational opportunities, and starting their own businesses. Because of their different countries of origin, different levels of acculturation, and consequential distinctive traits and characteristics, Hispanics present unique yet complex business opportunities for marketers. Still, there are core values to Hispanics that U.S. marketers need to be aware of if they want to target them as their customers.

Allocentrism (or collectivism): The tendency of Hispanics to put the group's welfare before their own personal welfare.

Familialism: Individuals' strong identification with and attachment to their nuclear and extended families and strong feelings of loyalty, reciprocity, and solidarity. This includes Hispanics providing (and accepting) material and emotional support to members of their extended family.

Simpatia: The need for behaviors that promote smooth and pleasant social relationships (engendering social harmony).

Power distance (personal respect): Respect and admiration for those perceived to have more power and authority.

Common Traits

While it is difficult to make generalizations about Hispanics, there exist some common traits:

Language: Hispanic immigrants are immediately exposed to the acculturation process, but they are assimilated at different speeds. Many continue to speak Spanish as their first language due to living in Hispanic neighborhoods where newspapers, televisions, signage, etc., are in Spanish.

Gender roles: While men tend to be the financial providers, women play a key role in home economics, thus in deciding how the family income is spent.

Family size: Hispanics tend to have three children, on average, and consider their extended family and even close friends and associates part of the family. "Mi casa es su casa" (my home is your home) is a sincere conviction and practiced tenet among Hispanics.

Residence: Most Hispanics (91%) live inside metropolitan areas in the West, South, and Northeast of the U.S.

Church affiliation: Many Hispanics are very involved with their local churches and participate in church social events.

Personal Space: Hispanics enjoy close physical contact with others in social situations.

Implications for Research

Of course, the values and traits cited above do not describe every Hispanic; however, they do provide insights into the community that have implications on market research. One of the greatest challenges is recruiting Hispanics to participate in market research studies. This is due to several factors, including wariness of people outside the extended family or community, concerns about releasing personal information about income or immigration status, unavailability on weekends due to family and church social events, and language barriers. To address these and other issues, researchers should consider the following:

- Survey samples should include both English-speaking and Spanish-speaking Hispanics in order to be representative of the U.S. Hispanic population.
- Survey translation must be accurate and culturally sensitive; involving Hispanic researchers and interviewers can help ensure this.
- For consumer packaged goods surveys, samples should be comprised of female heads of households, as they are the primary decision makers for these items.
- Programs should be developed and implemented to educate Hispanics about the benefits of market research. Incentives should benefit the family or community and not just the individual.
- Every effort should be made to create a positive survey experience, as positive word-of-mouth among Hispanics can be very powerful—and can help in recruiting additional Hispanic respondents.

THINGS YOU SHOULD HAVE BEEN TOLD WHEN YOU WERE IN THE 8TH GRADE…

Millionaire in the Making Basic Training in Investing

MIMT is geared towards conducting Basic Investment training beginning with youth in the junior high school level, gaining a consciousness of wealth, teaching them not to finish school with just a diploma and to go get a JOB (JUST OVER BROKE) but training them to become business owners, showing them how to own their own Franchise, acquainting youth with the basic knowledge of investment and to avoid the credit card trap of debt in life. Moreover, we want to train young minds understand early that investing is like a marriage, matching the right people to produce the highest yield in their future.

Young millionaires in the making cannot base relationships on lust, the way a person looks; one must make a proper assessment with counsel. Assess their education level, spending habits, the way they treat money, review there debt ratio to cash flow before partnering as a couple to avoid pitfalls in life. Each partner should review the other's CREDIT HISTORY. Please, don't start a relationship in debt, it's better to have a small inexpensive wedding, plan a honeymoon later with a higher cash flow, than to start with a high expensive wedding that will result in stress and debt. Study the relationships each partner had to ensure you are not becoming a part of their cycle. If there is a cycle of debt, still bound to bad relationships, had abuse issues in their past, you need to make a proper assessment. Your high school sweetheart may have the right football gear, but check his credit and brainpower! She may have the right curves, but check her past. These issues become blessing blockers.

You cannot build wealth without trust.

Before you go to war, get the right counsel. Most poor couples have more children than the rich couples; many poor people live in the projects yet drive a new Lexus and have a Bling Bling mentality.

Have a financial game plan.

This basic knowledge below will equip you to have a higher earning power rather than a higher spending power. Start day one with a game plan in the relationship. Create a game plan to increase your net worth, cut down liabilities, eating out, and movies every weekend, give 10% to tithes and 10% to yourself. The African American culture has the highest spending power with more consumers and less producers!! To get ahead, get a 2nd job, start your investment portfolio, invest today and start with the principles towards the end of this chapter (Strategies for Saving Money to Invest).

Many marriages end in a divorce because they were not matched properly and suited for each other. Many met on a one night stand, without proper counsel and took a high risk that yielded children and no real financial security. The couples were not trained in economics, were not taught how to form partnerships, and were not trained to buy their first home and to invest in stocks and bonds. A millionaire mindset starts with the knowledge about wealth, a basic understanding of mutual funds, stocks and bonds, CD's and other investment options. Knowledge is power. Unfortunately schools are not preparing youth to become entrepreneurs and many know more about sports then the Stock Market.

I will give you the ability to get wealth to establish the Kingdom. Kingdom Ambassador's should be trained to be positioned in life to have a seat at the New York Stock exchange which in today's dollar cost about 2 million dollars. Get your self in the position where you deserve to sit next to Warren Buffet, Bill Gates and Donald Trump. Stop thinking some one owes you something!

The American Stock Exchange (AMEX) is an American stock exchange situated in New York. AMEX is a mutual organization, owned by its members.

American Stock Exchange

The Exchange traces its roots back to colonial times when stock brokers created outdoor markets to trade new government securities. The AMEX started out as such a market at the curbstone on Broad Street near Exchange Place. The curb brokers gathered around the lamp posts and mail boxes, resisting wind and weather, putting up lists of stocks for sale. As trading activity increased, the shouting reached such a high level that special hand signals had to be introduced so that the brokers could continue trading. In 1921 the market was moved indoors into the building where it still resides, and the hand signals remained in place for decades even after the move.

AMEX's core business has shifted over the years from stocks to options, although it continues to trade small to mid-size stocks. An effort in the mid-1990s to initiate an Emerging Company Marketplace ended in failure, as the reduced listing standards (beyond the existing lenient AMEX standards) caused penny stock promoters to move their scams to a national exchange. In the mid 1990s the exchange was dogged by allegations of trading improprieties, which were highlighted by *BusinessWeek* in 1999.

In 1998, the American Stock Exchange merged with the National Association of Securities Dealers (operators of NASDAQ) to create "The Nasdaq-Amex Market Group" where AMEX is an independent entity of the NASD parent company. After tension between the NASD and AMEX members, the latter group bought out the NASD and acquired control of the AMEX in 2004.

Out of the three major American stock exchanges, the AMEX is known to have the most liberal policies concerning company listing, as most of its companies are generally smaller compared to the NYSE and NASDAQ. The Amex also specializes in the trading of ETFs, and hybrid/structured securities. The majority of US listed ETF's are traded at the AMEX including the SPDR and most Powershares.

In 2005, the AMEX attempted to popularize an American implimentation of the Canadian income trust model. Listed Equity Income Hybrid Securities, (more commonly known as Income Deposit Securities) listed on the AMEX are B & G Foods Holding Corp. (BGF), Centerplate, Inc. (CVP), Coinmach Service Corp. (DRY), and Otelco Inc. (OTT). Recently Coinmach Service Corp, has been attempting to restructure itself away from being an income trust.

The large companies listed on the AMEX include British American Tobacco (ADR)s, Imperial Oil Limited (IMO), Nabors Industries (NBR), Ivax Corporation (IVX) and Seaboard Corporation (SEB) and Bio-Rad Laboratories (BIO). Seaboard is notable for not having split its shares since becoming publicly listed, shares of SEB trade for around $1,600 a share.

Located next to the World Trade Center, it was affected by the September 11, 2001 attacks, but has recovered well since then.

New York Stock Exchange

New York Stock Exchange (June 2003)

The **New York Stock Exchange** (**NYSE**), also nicknamed the "**Big Board**", is the largest stock exchange in the world in dollar volume and second largest by number of companies listed. Its share volume was exceeded by that of NASDAQ (historic comparison graph - PDF) during the 1990s, but the total market capitalization of companies listed on the NYSE is five times that of companies listed on NASDAQ. The New York Stock Exchange has a global capitalization of $21 trillion, including $7.1 trillion in non-U.S. companies.

The NYSE is operated by NYSE Group, which was formed by merger with the fully electronic stock exchange Archipelago Holdings. The New York Stock Exchange trading floor is located at 11 Wall St., and is comprised of five rooms used for the facilitation of trading. The main building is located at 18 Broad Street, between the corners of Wall Street, and Exchange Pl., in New York City. The building is listed on the National Register of Historic Places.

Business

The NYSE trades in a continuous auction format. There is one specific location on the trading floor where each listed stock trades. Exchange members interested in buying and selling a particular stock on behalf of investors gather around the appropriate post where a specialist broker, who is employed by a NYSE member firm (that is, he/she is not an employee of the New York Stock Exchange), acts as an auctioneer in an open outcry auction market environment to bring buyers and sellers together and to manage the actual auction. They do on occasion facilitate the trades by committing their own capital (approximately 10% of the time) and as a matter of course disseminate information to the crowd that helps to bring buyers and sellers together. Most of the time natural buyers and sellers meet in a market that provides efficient price discovery in an auction environment that is designed to produce the fairest price for both parties. The human interaction and expert judgment as to order execution differentiates the NYSE from fully electronic markets. However, in excess of 50% of all order flow is now delivered to the floor electronically. Recent proposals have been made to adopt a Hybrid market structure combining elements of open outcry and electronic markets. The frenzied commotion of men and women in colored smocks has been captured in several movies, including *Wall Street*. Its main index, the Dow Jones Industrial Average, started life on October 1, 1928. It hit a peak on January 14, 2000 of 11,722,98. Since September 30, 1985 its trading hours have been 09:30 - 16:00 EST. The right to directly trade shares on the exchange is conferred upon owners of the 1366 "seats". The term comes from the fact that up until the 1870s NYSE members sat in chairs to trade; this system was removed long ago. In 1868, the number of seats was fixed at 533 and this number was increased several times over the years. In 1953, the exchange stopped at 1366 seats. These seats are a sought-after commodity as they confer the ability to directly trade stock on the NYSE. Seat prices have varied widely over the years, generally falling during recessions and rising during economic expansions. The most expensive seat was sold in 1929 for $625,000 which is over six million in today's dollars. In recent times, seats have sold for as high as $4 million in the late 1990s and $1 million in 2001. In 2005, seat prices shot up to $3.25 million as the exchange was set to merge with Archipelago and become a for-profit, publicly-traded company. Seat owners received $3.5 million cash per seat in the deal, and the NYSE now sells one-year licenses to trade directly on the exchange.

History

The origin of the NYSE can be traced to May 17, 1792 when the Buttonwood Agreement was signed by twenty-four stock brokers outside of 68 Wall Street in New York under a buttonwood tree. On March 8, 1817 the organization drafted a constitution and renamed itself the "New York Stock & Exchange Board". This name was shortened to its current form in 1863. Anthony Stockholm was elected the Exchange's first president.

U.S. Secretary of Commerce Donald L. Evans rings the opening bell at the NYSE on April 23, 2003. Former chairman Richard Grasso can also be seen in this picture.

The Exchange was closed shortly after the beginning of World War I (July 1914), but it was re-opened on November 28 of that year in order to help the war effort by trading bonds.

On September 16, 1920, a bomb exploded outside the NYSE building on Wall Street in a terrorist attack, killing 33 people and injuring more than 400. The perpetrators were never found. The NYSE building and some buildings nearby, such as the JP Morgan building, still have marks on their facades caused by the bombing.

The Black Thursday crash of the Exchange on October 24, 1929 and the sell-off panic which started on Black Tuesday, October 29, are often blamed for precipitating the Great Depression. In an effort to try to restore investor confidence, the Exchange unveiled a fifteen-point program aimed to upgrade protection for the investing public on October 31, 1938.

On October 1, 1934, the exchange was registered as a national securities exchange with the U.S. Securities and Exchange Commission, with a president and a thirty-three member board. On February 18, 1971 the not-for-profit corporation was formed, and the number of board members was reduced to twenty-five.

On August 24, 1967; Abbie Hoffman led a group opposed to capitalism (and other things, including the Vietnam War) in the gallery of the New York Stock Exchange. The protestors threw fistfuls of (mostly fake) dollar bills down to the traders below, who began to scramble frantically to grab the money, as fast as they could. Hoffman claimed to be pointing out that, metaphorically, that's what NYSE traders "were already doing". The NYSE then installed barriers in the gallery, to prevent this kind of protest from interfering with trading again.

On October 19, 1987, the Dow Jones Industrial Average fell 22.6%, one of the largest one-day declines in recorded stock market history. It has been dubbed "Black Monday."

Following a 554.26 point drop in the Dow Jones Industrial Average (DJIA) on October 27, 1997, officials at the Exchange for the first time invoked the "circuit breaker" rule to stop trading. This was a very controversial move and prompted a quick change in the rule; trading now halts for an hour, two hours, or the rest of the day when the DJIA drops 10, 20, or 30 percent, respectively. In the afternoon, the 10 and 20% drops will halt trading for a shorter period of time, but a 30% drop will always close the exchange for the day. The rationale behind the trading halt was to give investors a chance to cool off and reevaluate their positions (see the October 27, 1997 mini-crash).

The first central location of the NYSE was a room rented for $200 a month at 40 Wall Street in 1817.

Security around NYSE

The NYSE was closed from September 11 until September 17, 2001 as a result of the September 11, 2001 attacks.

On September 17, 2003, NYSE chairman and chief executive Richard Grasso stepped down as a result of controversy concerning the size of his deferred compensation package. He was replaced as CEO by John Thain, the former President of Goldman Sachs Group Inc.

On April 21, 2005, the NYSE announced its plans to acquire Archipelago, in a deal that is intended to bring the NYSE public.

On December 6, 2005, the NYSE's governing board voted to acquire rival Archipelago and become a for-profit, public company. It began trading under the name NYSE Group on March 8, 2006.

Marsh Carter is the Chairman of the New York Stock Exchange, succeeding John S. Reed. John Thain is the CEO of the NYSE and Catherine Kinney is the President of the NYSE.

Mutual Fund

A **mutual fund** is a portfolio of stocks, bonds, or other securities that is collectively owned by hundreds or thousands of investors and managed by a professional investment company. The shareholders are people who have similar investment goals. Each fund has specific investment criteria, which are spelled out in its **prospectus**, the official booklet that describes the mutual fund. Investors then know what they are getting and can match their objective to that of a fund. The pooled money has more buying power than one investor alone, so that a fund can own hundreds of different securities. Thus, its success is not dependent on how just one or two companies perform.

A mutual fund makes money in several ways: by earning dividends or interest on the investments it owns and by selling securities that have appreciated in value. You, in turn, make money in the form of dividends and interest that are passed on to you and the increase (or decrease) in the fund's value. The mutual fund manager keeps constant watch on financial markets and adjusts the portfolio to achieve the strongest returns. By owning part of a fund, the hard work of selecting and monitoring stocks and bonds is done for you.

A **mutual fund** is a portfolio of stocks, bonds, or other securities that is collectively owned by hundreds or thousands of investors and managed by a professional investment company. The shareholders are people who have similar investment goals. Each fund has specific investment criteria, which are spelled out in its **prospectus**, the official booklet that describes the mutual fund. Investors then know what they are getting and can match their objective to that of a fund. The pooled money has more buying power than one investor alone, so that a fund can own hundreds of different securities. Thus, its success is not dependent on how just one or two companies perform.

A mutual fund makes money in several ways: by earning dividends or interest on the investments it owns and by selling securities that have appreciated in value. You, in turn, make money in the form of dividends and interest that are passed on to you and the increase (or decrease) in the fund's value. The mutual fund manager keeps constant watch on financial markets and adjusts the portfolio to achieve the strongest returns. By owning part of a fund, the hard work of selecting and monitoring stocks and bonds is done for you.

Certificates of Deposit (CDs)?

Also known as "time deposits," certificates of deposit (CDs) are an insured bank product that pays a fixed rate of interest for a specified period of time (e.g., 18 months). Typical CD maturities range from seven days to five years, with higher rates of return paid on CDs with longer maturities. A penalty is assessed if funds are withdrawn prior to maturity, resulting in the loss of a certain number of days of interest (the amount varies among financial institutions). If an early withdrawal penalty exceeds the interest earned, the difference will be deducted from an investor's principal.

Many people think that CDs can only be purchased at banks. Many credit unions and full-service brokerage firms also sell federally insured CDs to investors. Investment firms purchase the CDs of banks nationwide in large blocks and sell them to investors in small denominations. The difference between their buying and selling price, called "the spread," is how they make a profit. Since brokers shop the entire country for high yields, brokered CDs often pay more attractive rates than CDs at local banks. CDs can be redeemed prior to maturity, often without penalty, but, due to interest rate risk, the value of a brokered CD can be higher or lower than someone's initial investment.

Another relatively new type of CD is the equity-indexed CD. Sold through both banks and brokers, these CDs base returns, in part, on appreciation of a stock market index like the Standard & Poor's 500 (S&P 500). Many require a $5,000 initial investment ($2,000 for IRAs). Unfortunately, equity-indexed CDs rarely include the full appreciation potential of the S&P 500 because they exclude the portion derived from company dividends. Many also cap the maximum growth rate, which further reduces upside potential. As a result, most financial advisors suggest avoiding these CDs and buying regular CDs for income and a stock index fund for capital growth.

Series EE and Series I U.S. Bonds

U.S. savings bonds are the lowest-denomination securities issued by the Federal government. Income earned is exempt from state and local taxes. Federal taxes can be deferred for up to 30 years or until the owner cashes a bond. Both the Series EE and I bond are available at most banks and many credit unions and other financial institutions in denominations ranging from $50 to $10,000. Many employers offer both Series EE and inflation-adjusted I Bonds through convenient payroll savings plans. The purchase price of EE Bonds is one-half their face value (e.g., $50 for a $100 bond). I bonds are sold at face value in the same denominations as Series EE. The accrued interest on both series is paid when the bonds are redeemed. Bonds can be redeemed at most financial institutions.

Series EE and Series I bonds must be held one year before being eligible for redemption. Redemptions prior to 5 years from issue are subject to a 3-month interest penalty (e.g., 21 months of interest for a bond cashed in after 24 months). Redemption values are available using the tables and Savings Bonds Wizard software available free at the Treasury Department Web site *http://www.savingsbonds.gov/* or by consulting tables available at most banks, credit unions and other financial institutions. You may also request a free table by writing to Bureau of the Public Debt, Savings Bond Operations Office, Parkersburg, WV 26106-1328.

Effective May 1, 2005, Series EE bonds pay a fixed interest rate for the life of the bond based on whatever rate is in effect at the time of purchase. Interest rate changes are made on May 1 and November 1. Series I Bonds earn a fixed rate over and above an inflation adjustment based upon changes in the Consumer Price Index. Interest accrues federally tax-deferred for as long as 30 years or until the bond is redeemed. Earnings on both series are subject to federal tax, but may be tax-free if cashed in a year when the owner pays qualified higher education expenses. Income limits and other restrictions apply; see IRS Form 8815 for details. Earnings from all savings bonds are exempt from state and local taxes. Current rate information can be obtained by phoning 1-800-4US-BOND (1-800-487-2663).

It is sometimes confusing to determine the current redemption value of Series EE bonds or when they have doubled in value. If interest rates are so low that a bond is not worth its face value in 17 years, the U.S. Treasury will add a one-time "make-up" to ensure that it is worth twice as much as an investor paid (e.g., $50 for a EE bond originally purchased for $25). Basic bond redemption tables are free and available at many banks or from the Bureau of the Public Debt, (see above). Another way to determine the value of a Series EE bond is to use the Savings Bond Wizard feature of the Treasury Department's Web site: *http://www.publicdebt.treas.gov/*. If your grandmother gave you a savings bond 20 years ago, for example, you can check a table or the Web site to find what it is worth.

There is also another U.S. savings bond available to investors: HH bonds. HH bonds are issued at full face value through an exchange of Series EE bonds, thus deferring federal income tax due on EE bond earnings for as long as 20 additional years. Denominations range from $500 to $10,000 and interest is paid semi-annually.

Money Market Mutual Funds

Money market mutual funds are a type of mutual fund consisting of high quality, short-term debt instruments such as Treasury bills and short term corporate IOUs. Like all mutual funds, money market mutual fund (MMMF) portfolios are professionally managed and a management fee is charged against fund assets to cover this expense. MMMFs offer market-based rates and are quick to respond to changing conditions because the average maturity of securities in their portfolio is 90 days or less. The minimum initial deposit is set by individual investment firms and can range from $250 to $25,000. MMMFs can be purchased directly from investment companies or with the assistance of financial advisors.

Unlike bank-sponsored money market deposit accounts (MMDAs), there is no FDIC insurance if a MMMF fails to maintain a $1 share price. Failures have happened very infrequently in the last 20 years, however, and most investment firms have shored up MMMF prices with other company assets to avoid a loss of principal by investors. Limited check writing is generally available on MMMFs with a minimum amount (e.g., $250) per check. Investors seeking both safety of principal and tax advantages can select tax-exempt MMMFs that include short-term securities issued by state and local governments. Other conservative choices are MMMFs that invest solely in Treasury bills and/or Treasuries plus debt of federal government agencies.

Bonds: An Overview

Before discussing various types of bonds, some background is in order. Bonds are debts or IOUs of corporations or government entities. Bond issuers promise to pay a specified rate of interest, called a coupon rate, periodically and to repay the face (a.k.a., par) value of the bond (e.g., $1,000) at **maturity**. Corporate and municipal bonds are typically sold by brokers, who receive a sales commission. Bonds are subject to **interest rate risk**. If interest rates rise, the value of previously issued bonds will drop as investors demand a price adjustment equivalent to earning the prevailing interest rate. If interest rates drop, a previously issued bond will be worth more than its face value because investors would be willing to pay a premium to obtain a bond paying more than the currently available rate. The value of long-term bonds is affected more than short-term bonds by interest rate fluctuations. Bonds are also subject to **call risk**. This means that a bond issuer may choose to retire existing bonds, issued when interest rates were high, and reissue them with new debt at a lower interest rate.

The capacity of bond issuers to repay their debt is rated by various commercial firms such as Moody's and Standard & Poor's. Bonds rated BAA to AAA by Moody's and BBB to AAA by Standard & Poor's are considered

investment grade. Those with lower ratings are termed substandard grade. Substandard grade bonds or bond funds can often be recognized by the words "junk" or "high yield" in their title.

U.S. Treasury Securities

Treasury securities are an obligation of the U.S. government and are considered the safest of all debt instruments because there has never been a default in payment. This concept is sometimes stated with the words "full faith and credit of the U.S. government." Treasury securities are sold at periodic government auctions, with fewer issues being sold recently because of the shrinking federal deficit. They are exempt from state and local income taxes due to the principal of reciprocal immunity. This means that the federal government doesn't tax state and local debt (e.g., municipal bonds) and state and local governments don't tax federal debt (e.g., Treasury Securities).

There are two types of Treasury securities currently available for purchase: bills and notes. All require a $1,000 minimum deposit with larger amounts purchased in increments of $1,000. Treasury bills have the shortest term of all Treasury securities and come in 3- and 6-month maturities. They are bought at a discount with investors paying $1,000 or more up front and receiving back an amount, called "the discount," equal to the interest rate determined by the most recent auction. At maturity, an investor's original purchase amount (principal) is returned. If interest rates are 4%, for example, an investor with $1,000 would receive a discount of $40 ($1,000 x 0.04) shortly after purchase and their $1,000 principal back at maturity.

Treasury notes currently come with 2-, 5-, and 10-year maturities. They pay a fixed rate of interest semi-annually until maturity, when investors get their principal back. For example, a $1,000, 5-year Treasury note with a 5% yield pays $25 every six months ($50 per year). The yield on Treasury notes is generally higher than that of bills to compensate for the risk of investing longer and the greater volatility that accompanies interest-rate changes.

Treasury securities can be purchased from a bank or brokerage firm for a fee of about $50 or with no fee from the Federal Reserve Bank's "Treasury Direct" program. An application, called a tender form, is required and can be obtained by calling 202-874-4000 for a list of Federal Reserve Banks or through the Treasury Department Web site *http://www.publicdebt.treas.gov/*. With Treasury Direct, an investor must specify a bank account where their interest payments can be deposited electronically. Treasury securities also can be sold through the Treasury Direct program for a nominal charge.

Municipal Bonds

Municipal bonds are debt instruments of state and local governments or government-related entities (e.g., bridge or highway authorities). **General obligation (GO) bonds** are backed by the full taxing ability of the issuer and are considered the safest of municipal bonds. A second type of municipal bond, the **revenue bond**, is backed by some type of revenue-generating source (e.g., fares, tolls, fees) and generally pays a slightly higher rate of return.

Municipal bonds are generally attractive to persons in the 27% (decreasing to 26% in 2004-05 and 25% in 2006) marginal tax bracket and higher. Even though municipal bonds pay a lower return than other bonds, investors keep more of what they earn because the interest is generally federally tax-exempt. Interest is also state tax-exempt, if bonds are issued by an investor's state of residence. An exception is the so-called private purpose municipal bond sold to finance sports stadiums, airports, hospitals, and the like. Municipal bonds are generally sold by brokerage firms in $5,000 increments with less expensive "minibonds" requiring a lower amount (e.g., $500). Interest is paid semi-annually. Investors can also obtain the tax advantages of a municipal bond by purchasing a municipal bond mutual fund, often for an initial investment of $1,000 or less. To determine your marginal tax bracket, refer to Figure 1 in Unit 7, "Tax-Deferred Investments".

Corporate Bonds

Corporate bonds are debt instruments issued by for-profit companies to raise capital for expansion and/or ongoing operations. They are generally sold in $1,000 increments and pay taxable interest twice a year. Corporate bonds generally pay higher interest rates than government bonds with comparable credit ratings and maturities. Investing in a corporation is a greater risk than a government entity that has the ability to raise revenue through taxes. Thus, investors must be compensated accordingly. The least risky of all corporate bonds is a **mortgage bond** because it is backed by a company's land and buildings. Bonds backed by non-real estate assets (e.g., airplanes, securities) have more risk. The highest risk corporate bond is a **debenture**, which is a corporate bond backed only by a company's future earnings and promises to repay. Conservative investors will want to select mortgage bonds issued by investment grade (i.e., highly rated) companies.

Convertible Bonds

As their name suggests, convertible bonds are a type of corporate bond that allows investors to "have their cake and eat it too," almost. They provide the upside potential of stocks (the opportunity to participate in company earnings) with the downside protection of bonds (a fixed return and repayment of principal at maturity). Convertible bonds can be exchanged for a specified number of shares of common stock of the issuing company. As the price of the company stock increases, the convertible bond price also increases because the option to convert becomes more valuable. This correlation is true whether an investor chooses to convert or not. The trade-off is that convertible bonds generally convert to fewer shares of stock than you could buy for the cost of a bond. Almost all convertible bonds are callable. Even though they are a "hybrid" investment, convertibles (like all bonds) are sensitive to interest rate fluctuations. They can be purchased as individual securities in $1,000 increments or through convertible bond mutual funds.

Zero-Coupon Bonds

As their name implies, zero-coupon bonds pay no (zero) annual interest. Instead, they are sold at a deep discount and eventually grow to full face value ($1,000). An investor might pay only $200 or $300, for example, for a bond that matures in 15 or 20 years. Brokers may require a $5,000 purchase, however, or five times the initial cost. For example, an 8% zero-coupon bond with 15 years to maturity would cost $308. To purchase five such bonds ($5,000 face value) would cost $1,540 (5 x $308). So, in this example, if you invest $1,540 now, you know you'll get back $5,000 in 15 years. This return might be suitable for a goal you want to achieve in 15 years (e.g., future education expenses of a young child).

Many investors like zero-coupon bonds for their relatively low upfront cost and predictability. An investor knows exactly how much they'll have at maturity. Two disadvantages of zero-coupon bonds are their extreme volatility with interest rate changes and the fact that annual increases in value are considered taxable income. Immediate taxation can be avoided, however, by using zero-coupon bonds for tax-deferred retirement plans, such as IRAs, or by buying tax-exempt (e.g., municipal) zero-coupon municipal bonds.

Unit Investment Trusts

Unit Investment Trusts (UITs) are a professionally selected portfolio of similar securities (e.g., 30-year municipal bonds) packaged together and sold by brokerage firms. Unlike mutual funds, UITs are a "buy and hold" investment, and there is no ongoing portfolio management. UIT sponsors simply buy a collection of bonds (and, with some UITs, stocks) and hold them. Investors receive periodic interest payments and a return of principal at maturity. If bonds within a UIT portfolio are sold or called prior to maturity, some principal may be returned sooner.

UITs are generally sold in $1,000 increments called units. The interest earned is taxable unless a UIT invests in tax-exempt bonds. If an investor needs his/her money prior to maturity, units can be redeemed at their current market value, subject to interest rate risk. Two advantages of UITs are broad diversification and steady cash flow. A specified rate of return is locked in for the duration of a UIT. Two disadvantages are high upfront costs (typically a 3% to 5%

sales charge) and the potential for loss if units are sold prior to maturity. For some UITs, selling units prior to maturity may be difficult or costly because secondary markets are small. For more information on UITs, see Unit 8.

Bond Mutual Funds

Instead of purchasing individual securities, an investor might decide to purchase shares of a bond mutual fund. Advantages include broad diversification, liquidity, and ongoing professional management. In addition, bond fund accounts can sometimes be opened for $500 or less, making them attractive for persons with small dollar amounts to invest. The biggest disadvantage of bond mutual funds is that, unlike individual securities and UITs, there is no fixed maturity date. Thus, the price of shares is always subject to fluctuation with changes in interest rates, and an investor could lose principal if interest rates increase. As with all mutual funds, the key factors to look for when selecting a bond fund are historical performance and expenses. Unlike stock funds, that have the potential for capital appreciation to offset fund expenses, bond funds must rely on low management costs to enhance their returns. In addition, bond funds generally invest in similar securities (e.g., Treasuries), so most of the difference in return among bond funds is due to differences in cost. The average annual expense ratio (expenses as a percentage of fund assets) for bond funds is about 1% ($1 for every $100 invested), but there are some low-cost fund families like Vanguard, T.Rowe Price, TIAA-CREF, and Fidelity that charge significantly less.

A 1997 study of bond mutual funds by *Consumer Reports* magazine found that, among government bond funds, funds with low expense ratios outperformed their peers. One low-cost bond mutual fund is a bond index fund. Bond index funds purchase the same securities that comprise a benchmark bond index, such as the Lehman Brothers Aggregate. Since the portfolio of securities is pre-determined by whatever bonds comprise an index, trading costs are minimal and bond index fund management expenses are low. Like individual bonds, bond funds with the longest maturities are extremely volatile when interest rates fluctuate. Conservative investors should select short-term bond funds consisting of investment grade securities.

Mortgage-Backed Securities

Mortgage-backed securities are investments in a portfolio of home mortgages and are sometimes referred to as "pass-through" securities because homeowners' mortgage principal and interest payments are "passed through" to investors. The most well-known mortgage-backed security is the Ginnie Mae, which is issued by the Government National Mortgage Association (GNMA). Ginnie Maes carry the "full faith and credit" guarantee of the federal government. Ginnie Maes require a $25,000 minimum purchase, with $5,000 increments, from brokers, but can also be purchased indirectly for $1,000 through units in a Ginnie Mae unit investment trust. They can also be purchased through mutual funds that invest in U.S. government agency securities (minimum amounts vary per fund).

Two other mortgage-backed securities that are not backed by the federal government are Freddie Macs, issued by the Federal Home Loan Mortgage Corporation (FHLMC) and Fannie Maes, issued by the Federal National Mortgage Association (FNMA). They also require $25,000 and typically pay a higher rate than Ginnie Maes to compensate investors for the extra risk of not being government-insured.

The biggest disadvantages of all three mortgage-backed securities are an uncertain maturity and irregular monthly payments. Although the mortgages in their portfolios are issued for 30 years, the average life of a mortgage-backed security is only 10 to 12 years because homeowners frequently move or refinance. Also, if investors spend the part of their monthly check that is a return of principal, instead of reinvesting it, they will have nothing left when the last mortgage in their Ginnie Mae portfolio is repaid.

Collateralized Mortgage Obligations

Collateralized mortgage obligations (CMOs) are another type of mortgage-backed security. CMOs were developed to address investors' concern about receiving income from other mortgage-backed securities in unpredictable increments. With CMOs, the portfolio of mortgages is divided into various classes, called tranches, thus offering investors a choice of estimated maturity dates to match financial goals. Investors in a particular tranche receive periodic income payments (typically monthly) that differ from period-to-period and from other tranches. Tranches with a longer maturity generally pay a higher return to compensate investors for incurring greater interest rate risk. The principal portion of mortgage payments corresponding to all tranches goes to investors in a single tranche until that tranche is retired. Each tranche gets its principal back when all the tranches before it have been repaid. CMOs are available in $1,000 increments through brokerage firms and pay a higher yield than comparable mortgage-backed securities. Two disadvantages are their complexity and the fact that principal prepayment can still come sooner (or later) than expected. Just as with other mortgage-backed securities, investors must realize that principal is being repaid throughout the life of a CMO, not at maturity like bonds. Investors who mistakenly think that CMO payments are just interest may inadvertently spend their principal.

Annuities

An annuity is a contract with an insurance company to provide regular income immediately or at some time in the future for a specified period (e.g., the lifetime of an annuitant or an annuitant and his/her spouse), typically during retirement years. In return, an investor deposits a sum of money with an insurance company, which grows tax-deferred until withdrawal, or makes periodic payments. There are two types of annuities: **variable annuities** which provide access to growth-oriented (ownership) and income-oriented (loanership) investments through a choice of mutual fund subaccounts, and **fixed annuities** that guarantee a fixed rate of return for a specified period of time. Thus, fixed annuities are like a CD, but are tax-deferred. A rate of return is locked in for a period of 1 to 5 years after purchase and then adjusted annually according to market conditions. Annuities generally require a $5,000 minimum investment. Annuity investors should compare surrender charges (a fee assessed for cashing out early), rates of return, and the financial health of insurance companies that offer annuities. Be sure to check with rating services such as A.M. Best, Moody's, and Duff and Phelps and stick with top-rated insurance companies.

Preferred Stock

Although technically a form of stock, preferred stock is often listed as a fixed-income investment because it behaves more like a bond, but has no fixed maturity date. The word "preferred" refers to the fact that shareholders receive preferential treatment. They are paid dividends before common stock shareholders and, in the event of a corporate liquidation, can claim corporate assets after bondholders but before common stock shareholders. Preferred stock typically pays a fixed dividend rate similar to the coupon rate on a bond. Share prices fluctuate inversely with changes in interest rates. Par value on preferred stock is usually about $25 per share so a round lot (100 shares) would cost $2,500. Dividends paid are a fixed percentage of par value. Preferred stock shares are available through brokerage firms.

Guaranteed Investment Contracts

Called GICs for short, guaranteed investment contracts are fixed-income contracts issued by insurance companies as an investment option for 401(k) retirement plans. Another, more commonly used, name for GICs is "stable value funds." Like CDs, only tax-deferred, GICs pay a fixed-interest rate for a specified period of time (e.g. 3 to 5 years). Because they are backed by an insurance company, and not the federal government, GICs generally pay a higher return than CDs and other cash investments. Their return is lower than stocks, however, leading to criticism that they are inappropriate for long-term financial goals like retirement.

Wealth Protection

Cash Management

Cash management strategies include budgeting, keeping financial records, maximizing the interest earned on checking and savings accounts, and regularly preparing financial statements, such as net worth and cash flow. One of the soundest pieces of financial advice is to spend less than you earn. It sounds simple, but if you are not fully aware of how you spend money, you may be spending more than you realize. After you track your income and expenses, following a budget that is adjusted to your individual situation and goals is an excellent strategy to plan your spending.

To estimate the value of your assets and chart your financial progress, each year you should add together everything you own (assets), then subtract everything you owe (debts), including your mortgage and credit card debt. This summary of assets and debts is called a **net worth statement** or **balance sheet**. It will help you analyze the way you currently manage your finances and make decisions to improve your financial situation.

You want your net worth to increase each year. During the early stages of your life, when you're establishing yourself at work and accumulating the necessities of life, your net worth may rise slowly. It will probably grow the most right before retirement when you are at the peak of your career and accumulating assets to ensure a secure retirement. Plan to review and update your net worth annually. The actual date of your review is not important. It might be your birthday, New Year's, right after you do your taxes, or some other important date. It is more important that you remember the date and complete your annual checkup. It also is important to regularly reconcile bank and other financial statements with your own records.

A vital aspect of the cash management building block is financial record-keeping. An effective record-keeping system should be convenient and not too complicated to maintain. A number of systems are available commercially, or you can design your own (e.g., with file folders). It is important that the system makes sense to you and that you use it consistently.

Emergency Cash Reserve

Setting aside money to meet unexpected expenses provides a financial safety net and allows you to take advantage of financial opportunities as they arise. Most experts recommend an **emergency fund** equal to 3 to 6 months living expenses; however, you do not need to set aside this total amount in a low-yielding passbook, certificate of deposit, or money market account. The amount of your emergency fund depends upon your age, health, job outlook, and personal financial situation (e.g., amount and kind of insurance coverage). An emergency fund might be adequate with enough to cover 3 to 6 months of expenses using a combination of cash and credit if you have a source of low-cost borrowing (e.g., home equity credit-line loan, cash-value life insurance, or retirement plan). If your household has multiple sources of income or dual earners, you can count on those other sources of income in an emergency.

You might want a larger emergency fund if you are in business for yourself, your work is seasonal, your job is uncertain, or you rely heavily on commissions. If your health is questionable (e.g., you foresee long-term disability or extensive medical expenses), you anticipate a large expenditure for the care of a relative in the near future, or your child is about to enter college, you may also need a larger cash reserve.

Your emergency cash reserve can be subdivided to minimize penalties for early withdrawal of large amounts of funds at one time and to maximize interest earned on accounts should an emergency occur. Money that would be needed within 3 months of a financial emergency is best placed in an interest-bearing checking account, passbook savings, money-market deposit account, or money market mutual fund. Funds needed 4 to 6 months after an emergency could be placed in short-term certificates of deposit (CDs) as well as 3- and 6-month Treasury bills. Money that would not be needed for 7 months to 2 years could be placed in a money market mutual fund and longer term CDs (12-, 18-, and 24-month). Money you can avoid withdrawing for 2 to 5 years during a financial emergency could be placed in Treasury notes, short-term bond funds, or 3- to 5-year CDs.

Are You Satisfied with the Amount You Save?

This unit is designed to help you "find" money to fund your investment plans. We will suggest tools for success, but you have to supply the desire, self-discipline, wise decisions, and good planning to be successful.

Review your financial status by answering these questions:

- Do I have 3 to 6 months income in an emergency fund?
- Do I save regularly?
- Do I know how much I need to save to achieve future goals?
- Do I save to purchase big-ticket items instead of buying on credit?
- When I use credit, do I save to make as large a down payment as possible?
- Do I save at least 10% of my personal disposable income?
- Do I know how much I need to save for retirement?

The more times you answer "yes" to these questions, the more likely you are a prudent saver. A "no" can help you identify areas where you could do better. Once you have a sound savings program in place, you are ready to invest surplus funds. Unfortunately, many people feel their savings are not sufficient, and they see no way to meet their immediate needs and have extra funds to invest.

Through this unit of study, you will explore strategies that will help you:

1. Identify ways to increase your savings
2. Fund your savings program
3. Accumulate funds to begin your investment program.

It doesn't take a lot of money to start investing. Unit 8, *Investing With Small Dollar Amounts*, provides examples of investments that require as little as $25 for a U.S. savings bond or $250, $500, or $1,000 to open a mutual fund account, depending on account requirements.

Strategies for Saving Money to Invest

Establish a Regular Savings Program

The first strategy is to set up a regular savings program if you do not already have one. Saving means putting money aside from present earnings to provide for a known or unexpected need in the future. It is an integral part of family and personal financial planning. Having a specific goal provides motivation to save. You probably will not get very far saving for the sake of saving.

Needs versus Wants

Individuals and families save to satisfy their needs and wants. **Needs** are items that are necessary for survival such as food, shelter, clothing, and medical care. **Wants** are all the other things we think we need, but could do without. If we spend our money to satisfy wants before we meet our needs, we will probably experience financial difficulties. The pressure to acquire present wants is often greater than the willingness to provide for future needs or even future wants.

Generally speaking, four major financial needs require planning for in the near and distant future:

1. **Emergencies** from the normal course of living such as car repairs or replacing a major appliance
2. **Loss of income** as a result of death, divorce, disability, or unemployment
3. **Other family goals** such as education for your children or a special vacation
4. **Retirement**

Once goals have been set, a major thought in most people's minds is "How am I going to reach this goal? There is no way I can save that much money!"

However, most people find that, if they really put their minds to it and they have set realistic goals, they can save the necessary money.

As we noted earlier, a regular savings program is critical to a family's immediate well-being as well as their long-term security. To adequately fund a savings program and begin an investment program, you must identify a specific amount to save from each paycheck and honor that commitment. Regular savings in small amounts is generally more effective than setting aside larger sums at sporadic intervals. As your salary increases, increase the amount you commit to savings.

Pay Yourself First

Another important concept for your savings program is to "pay yourself first." Make your "savings bill" a part of your spending plan, just like rent or mortgage payments, utility bills, clothing, car payments and upkeep, child care, or any other bill that you normally incur. When you pay your other bills, pay your savings bill by depositing the money into a savings account or other financial instrument. One painless way to accomplish this is payroll deduction if it is available. Your employer deposits your savings directly from your paycheck into a credit union, bank account, or a money market fund for a higher interest rate. If you never see the money, you won't miss it or be tempted to use it for something else before it reaches your savings account. Note how quickly small amounts of money can grow with time

Mutual Funds: 10 Advantages

1. You get **full-time, professional money management**. Most people do not have the time or skill to select and monitor individual stocks and bonds.

2. You get **reduced risk through diversification** because a mutual fund owns many stocks or bonds. You can also pick your level of market risk by choosing particular types of funds (e.g., money market funds to insure your principal will not drop in value, bond funds if you want current income and some stability in your portfolio, stock funds if you want your money to grow over the long term.)

3. You will earn **competitive returns** on your investment. Mutual funds can furnish the kinds of returns you need to reach your goals. In fact, by choosing an index fund, (a fund that invests in securities of one of the broadly based market indexes such as Standard and Poor's 500), you can expect to match the market's performance, minus the expenses of running the fund. This is an assurance that no other investment can provide.

4. **You don't need a lot of money to get started.** Many funds require only

$1,000 to open an account, and some funds require minimum initial investments as low as $250 to $500. Subsequent deposits can be as small as $25 to $100 if an **automatic investment plan** (AIP) is adopted. An AIP is an arrangement where you agree to have money automatically withdrawn from your bank account on a regular basis, (e.g., once a month or every quarter) and used to purchase fund shares.

5. You retain **ready access to your money**. A mutual fund is required to buy back your shares, which makes withdrawals easy. It will mail your check within seven days of the request at the closing price (NAV) on the day it is received. (An exception to receiving NAV at sale time is back-end load funds that charge a redemption fee).

6. Mutual funds are a **cheaper** way to get the investing job done. Research and operating costs are shared by the thousands of shareholders. The most efficiently run funds have an **expense ratio** (the percentage of fund assets deducted for management and operating expenses) of less than 1% a year. Some well-established funds charge annual fees as low as 0.2% to 0.5%. Also, many funds are sold directly through their sponsors with no sales charge-known as "no-load" funds. Funds that charge a sales commission are called "load" funds.

7. Mutual funds are **convenient**. They can be purchased (and sold) directly from a mutual fund company by mail and by telephone and from full-service brokers, financial planners, banks or insurance companies. (*Important note: when mutual funds are purchased from banks, they are not insured by the FDIC like other bank products.)* In addition, some discount brokers have established mutual fund "supermarkets" where investors can own funds from many different fund families in one consolidated account without any sales charges or transaction fees. Earnings from mutual funds can also be automatically reinvested in additional shares. Reinvesting and compounding are keys to building wealth.

8. **Automatic withdrawal plans are available**, making it possible to have a steady stream of income for retirement (e.g., withdrawals of $250 per month).

9. Mutual funds have **less risk of bankruptcy or fraud** than many other securities because they are highly regulated by the federal government through the SEC, which is charged with assuring that mutual funds and investment advisors follow specific rules of disclosure.

10. **Monitoring mutual funds is simple.** Prices are reported daily in the financial section of many newspapers and more in-depth information is available in the Sunday business sections (See the WALLSTREET JOURNAL)

MIMT Millionaires in the Making Basic sessions are held purposely to unlock the genetically infinite abilities within man that need to be awakened. Untapped potentials have been limited through the negative sabotaging energy, beliefs, and mental conditioning that have poisoned the soul. MITM trainings are held at the request of Training and we ask you to invite us to your organization, church, school, or college. We believe that we can change the complexities of the world by changing one consciousness at a time. Thru Positive Psychological re-imaging programs, many lives have already been changed.

CHAPTER 5

Millionaire's Shift in Consciousness
The Symbol of Money

What would do if I had a Million Dollars?

This story proves the truth that when you shift in consciousness you will manifest your desire and realize you have an eternal purpose, a higher purpose in life.

If you were given a million dollars, what will you do with it? Dr. Gunsaulus was going through college, where he could carry out his ideas without being handicapped by orthodox methods of education. He needed a million dollars to put this project across. Where would this money come from? This question absorbed most of his waking moments, until he realize he needed to take *action* toward his dream. He made up in his mind that he would receive the money in a couple of weeks; ***he had definite purpose.***

He called the newspapers and announced he would preach a sermon the following morning on "What I would do if I had a Million Dollars." He went to sleep with a feeling of confidence that he saw himself already in possession of the million dollars. The next Sunday morning after preaching the message, a man name Phillip D. Armour walked up to him after service, asked him to come to his office the next day, and gave him the necessary funding to start his company, the Armour Institute of Technology.

"A computer in every desk in every home." Bill Gates

"A Millionaire Status manual in the hand of all humans from 8 to 80 to change the Faces of poverty." —Israel Prince

The Universe is user friendly

The Universe is not like people it is user friendly, it will release the exact images, pictures, imprints of your mind and place an ideal in your mind!

Television shows all over America have captivated us, such as *Who Wants to be a Millionaire.* A tangible millionaire is one who is considered a very wealthy person, one whose value is at least one thousand dollars. On becoming a millionaire, certainly this begins with a consciousness of prosperity and a hot pursuit to serve the world with a proven product! It doesn't matter whether you take on the perishables of a Famous Amos, the modeling of a Madame CJ. Walker, or duplicate the media building design of a Ted Turner, if you start with the premises of serving people, then you will win. The universe has plenty; lavish abundance is all around us. You must first be convinced within, mentally.

Attend a Millionaires in Training Seminar in your city. They are designed to dethrone the negatives blueprints conditioning within individuals who have been trained to repel wealth instead of attracting wealth. This is why those who win the lottery in one year return to a poverty lifestyle; they failed to destroy the negative gatekeepers in their mind.

Psychosomatic Induced

Medical doctors and tacticians have documented that most sickness, illness, depression, frustrations is a direct result of a psychosomatic self-induced disease of the mind. When one thinks a certain way, it releases certain chemical from the brain which cause a person to react a certain way, physiology jams the apostle put it this way 'life and death is in the power of the tongue.'

If one changes first his thought processes then he will change his outward world. Your thoughts create reality. We learn here that the amount of zeros behind your salary is a direct belief of your worth. Many children have inherited a wealth conscious. Other inherited a poverty consciousness.

Law of Physics

The only difference of silver and gold is the amount of rotation around the nucleus. At a certain rate of motion metals change there molecular structure. You can vibrate rich wealthy thoughts at a certain rate to where you will attract wealth and riches. Fill your mind with rich thoughts. Confess I am a money magnet! Think and grow rich!

Whatever state we are in is a direct result of our early childhood conditioning (belief system). On becoming a millionaire, firstly has nothing to do with the tangible substances of money, it has all to do with environmental conditioning and ideals, myths, beliefs and speech in regards to money. It has to do with the visible is made by the invisible. Remember Hebrew 11:1 faith is the substance of things hoped for, the evidences of things not seen.

The divine substance of prosperity and wealth is hidden inside of you. Inside of you is the wisdom of the ages. Inside of you is the divine substance of reality. You have got to go imagine yourself rich, feel rich, taste the riches. Associate with the rich. Stop being cursed by your kinfolks. You intimidate them with your riches; they ask you who do you think you are. Tell them you are a child of royalty. Thoughts produce things.

Jesus said, 'a good man will produce God things out of the good treasures of his heart! '

God had so many dreams that the angels in heaven couldn't figure out what to do. The ideal came to make millions of men who could walk out his dreams. We arc fulfilling the dreams of God. That's why when you have a dream, you need friends; you cannot fulfill your dream by yourself. You have to develop a likeable spirit, create a positive self-image, dress for success, radiate joy and celebrate other dreams. Believe you can become a millionaire, unlock the millions of possibilities within you.

Begin where you are. Begin now!

Millionaire Status Principle #38

To come into the fullness of millionaire status, one must awake the genius within, release prior conditioning, negative habits, attitudes, and all dispositions that will repel riches and wealth.

Trust God for the right ideals; right divine relationships, pray for your creative powers to be released. Ask for angelic help. Have a burning desire and never quit!

Millionaires of the Bible

Do you have a religious negative programming which repels wealth, new money and happiness? Solomon got in such a position in mind, that whatever he requested God granted it unto him!

Generations of good Christians have lived in poverty, under a generational curse, never manifesting their dreams, many who were called as business entrepreneurs, yet never to see their dreams due their religion programmed them to despise money. They were conditioned to see their preacher ride in a Cadillac with spinners on it, having a bling bling mentality, while they were on section 8, food stamps, welfare roll, it's time to destroy that religious lie. Our organization through this book purpose to make every one in the pews a millionaire!

The first calling of the Bible is to practice networking with the world. We live on a planet with over 400 billions people to market your dream to, you have the ability, you have the dominion seed, and you came in the earth as a Millionaire in the making. God said for you to have dominion, not working from paycheck to paycheck, worrying about debt, bills, bankruptcy, and living in a shack all your life.

Millionaire Status Principle #39

You have to market, manufacture, develop, and sell your gift to the world! Make thyself in demand! Thou shall meditate day and night, make the dream a reality! Believe in the dream, even if the whole world doesn't believe! With over 400 billion people on the planet, what if only 10% bought into your dream?? In my city Seattle, a METROPLEX, that has 1.7 million people; I only need 1% of this to be successful! Sell 1 % of cakes, 1 % of books, 1 % of houses, 1 % of popcorn, you will be rich! Stop worrying about the crowd who won't buy into your dream, you carry it, you birth it! Use the internet, radio, TV, cell phone, Ipod, satellites, CD's, DVD's, get your dream out to the world's market! There are 52 states in the US go to the ends of the world, market overseas, but don't give up on your dream!

Market your GIFT to the World!

Genesis is the book of new beginnings, if you desire a new beginning, then you need a fresh revelation on Kingdom. 85% of the churches in America preach a wait til you die gospel that Jesus never preached. Jesus preached Kingdom, the rule, the reign of God in all levels of your life.

Genesis 1:26 states the DOMINION MANDATE , the divine Call of ENTREPRENEURS in the earth, God never design you to work a 9-5, to work 25 years waiting on a pension, God never intended you to live, work and die in an EGYPTIAN SYSTEM. You have to shift to Kingdom!

Deuteronomy 8:18 But thou shall remember the Lord thy God***, for it is he that give thee the POWER to get wealth!***

Imagine Riches

Let's make a man in our image to have dominion, to have the control of your destiny, your time, you determine how many zero's behind your paycheck. God cuts a covenant of dominion to institute him program in the earth, which needs no support form an Egyptian system. This is why the word came to our organization to begin the, "Millionaire in Training Seminars," to equip individuals with the skills, the strategies to become entrepreneurs. You must have a millionaire mindset, millionaire images in your consciousness, a rich blueprint, you become your most dominate thought.

There has been such a misrepresentation of kingdom living in the church. For years I was trained to believe that Jesus was poor, that he closed his eyes and found 12 poor derelicts that had nothing to do but start his storefront church. I found thru study and revelation of the word that the bible is a book of millionaires.

Millionaire Daniel

Daniel a great prophet of the tribe of Judah, who was taken captive to Babylon, he was renamed Belteshazzar by the King of Babylon, Daniel was superior in wisdom and knowledge and understanding above al the magician and seers in the whole Babylonian realm. Daniel had understanding in all visions and dreams, he purpose in his heart not to defile himself with the KINGS MEAT!

Daniel was a high officer of the Babylon Empire throughout its 70 years; Darius the conqueror of Babylonian placed Daniel in charge of the Government. The infinite wisdom and miracles which Daniel wrought had a prophetic influence on both Nebuchadnezzar and Darius. Daniel was bestowed the authority being of the Chief adviser of Nebuchadnezzar, who was the genius, real builder of the Babylonian Empire. In Daniel's day, the city of Babylon not only was the premier city of the pre-Christian world, it ruled the most powerful empire up till that time. Daniel was more than a millionaire; he was the first of the presidents in command of this great city.

Daniel 6 1-4

It pleased the King Darius to set over the KINGDOM an hundred and twenty princes, which should be over the whole kingdom, and over these presidents of whom Daniel was first, that the princes might give account unto them, and the King have no damages, then this Daniel was preferred ABOVE the president and princes, because an EXCELLENT spirit was in him, and the king though to set him over the entire realm.

Millionaire Abraham

Genesis 13:2 **Abraham** was very rich in cattle, in silver and in gold. Abraham practiced the laws of creating wealth. In Genesis 24: 14 Abraham servants declared the lord has made my master rich. Historians have described Abraham as a prophet of God, who belonged to a wealthy Babylonian family; Abraham was a pioneer, prepared the way for others to follow. Abraham was told by God , I will bless you and make you a blessing, he had to come out of his old mindset, his old country, he had to leave kinfolks alone, he had to deliver himself form negative energy, negative vibration which would have kill his dream. Abraham held fast to the Vision, he walked out each night and imagine his seed being as the stars in the heavens, he became the father of faith by staying in an EXALTED STATE. He exercises dominion over his domain.

The universe could not manifest the expanded consciousness until in Genesis 13, he got rid of LOT.

LOT represent anything, any person, any ideal that locking up your demonstration of supreme permanent wealth, new money and abundances.

Lot represents the negative side of man. GET RID OF LOTS!!! The Lots could be past pains, past relationships or unforgiveness.

Genesis 13:14 reveals that until you release the lots in your life, you're good cannot manifest! You cannot go forward, your business will not grow with a LOT in it, your family will not prosper, your church will split with a LOT in it, let LOT go!!

And the Lord said unto Abraham, after LOT WAS SEPARATED FROM HIM! I try to bring you into the land of prosperity, the land of milk and honey, land of divine overflow.

After Lot was separated from him, lift up now thy eyes, look from the place where thou art, eastward, westward, southward and northward, for al the land you see will I give to thee and thy seed! And I will make thy seed as the DUST OF THE EARTH, so that no man can number them.

Get rid of Lot, *then go forward and possess your Canaan land! Go forward into the place of JABEZ; go forward into the place of REHOBOTH! PLACE OF EXPANSION!*

Millionaire Isaac

"The man with a shovel digging new wells of opportunities"

In the past when I was the Director of a day-care and Principal of a k-12 grade academy, our organization needed more space; this presented a problem outwardly (if you desire rain, then wear a raincoat even if the meteorologist's forecasts hot weather). Many of the members asked why there was a shovel in front of the church; I responded that we are getting ready to move. Movement starts in the mind then manifests in the reality! The shovel represented that our old well was not dry. Sometimes you just need to dig a little deeper, and there is water underneath the myriads of lack. I was lead to place a shovel in front of our building, the Holy Spirit said "I will give new life, dig again." We experienced not only new life, but a larger location and prosperity abounded. Once you master your present, then you will demonstrate more in your future. Instead of running from your situation, arguing, complaining, hanging your harps on the willow tree, master the circumstances, learn to walk on water, above the opinions of folks, doubters, unbelievers and land your first million dollar break thru to your oil well.

The universe desire to raise up a few Spiritual NAVY SEALS, a few Militants Marines, astronauts who will walk in places where other are afraid, Invent, design, discover, create, new frontiers, new paradigms, a few 3rd Millennium Entrepreneur Rangers who will fight in spite of defeat, a few who will join the Gideon Army and pull back , but forge ahead in imagination, in faith and Conquerors there dreams! Let go of your fears, anxieties, where you are going, spirit has already ordered you steps, step out of debt, into abundance.

We were directed to move to the other side of town, sometime you prosperity is in relocation not closure. When you see an end, divine intelligence declares a new birth!

Isaac, means joy, laughter, happiness and peace. Isaac was born after Sarah was past the age for bringing forth, besides she was barren, there was no possibility of conception under the natural course of things.

As you sow the rich imagination, the prosperous consciousness, you to will conceive after others declare your dream will never happen, COME INTO THE ISAAC FLOW, where you will experience new life, a new flow after a bad relationship, after a ruin business, after the crowd declare you impotent, God will give you laughter! Poor people work for money; the rich become the symbol of money. When you show us, you represent the symbol of wealth, affluence, influence, no longer working for money, you are money! When you release these words into the ethers of times, the vibrations releases a force into the universe attracting that which is like substance within you, that why poor people stay poor, they fail to change the stuff on the inside, you only attract more of what lies within you!

Isaac inherited the rich wealthy spirit from Abraham, in spite of his fathers' demonstration he manifested wealth himself by utilizing the laws of prosperity which he had been trained in. He learned to stay in an elegant, luxury, beautiful, rich mindset even when his surrounding was a desert place. He continued to magnetize wealth, Isaac knew the powers of the mind, and he activated them, refused to get in a poverty state.

Isaac prospers even in a desert place. He understood that Gerar meant a halting place, not a permanent dwelling place, it was a place of inward growth to dig new wells of prosperity, to concentrate on more riches and not get hypnotize by the appearance of lack, there was a famine!

COME TO YOUR 'REHOBOTH!

*God brought him into his '**Rehoboth**' broad places, wide streets, market places, and the place of expansion, enlargement and prosperity. Place where there is plenty of room, no more living In the projects, no more living from paycheck to paycheck, no more stressing over low finances, no more Goodwill clothes, Now you can shop at Macy's, buy handbags from Louis Vuitton, Versace , travel to Beverly Hill to Rodeo Drive, enjoy the finest living , most celebrated clothing lines, Armani, Gucci, Christian Dior, Ralph Lauren, Valentino, shop at Neiman Marcus!*

Genesis 26:1

And there **was a famine in the** land, besides the first famine that was in the days of Abraham, Isaac went unto Abimelech king of the Philistines unto Gerar. Gerar in Greek means a sojourn, a lodging place, an encampment, a halting place. It was here that Isaac herdsmen and the herdsmen of Gerar contended over the wells that Isaac servants dug.

And the Lord appeared unto him, and said, **Go not down to Egypt, (don't go back to your past) IT'S A NEW SEASON. Dwell in the land (mentality, consciousness, and place)** where I have assigned you! Sojourn in this land and I will be with thee and I will bless thee, I will increase thee, I will cause you to come into a divine overflow blessings! Of unto thee and unto thy seed I will give ALL THESE COUNTRIES, I will perform the oath which I swore unto Abraham thy father. Isaac received the divine overflow blessing due e he stayed connected to his father's flow! I will make thy seed to multiply as the stars of the heavens, I will give unto thy seed all these countries, and in thy seed shall all the nations of the earth be blessed! Because ABRAHAM OBEYED my voice and kept my covenant, my charge, my statutes and laws.

God told Abraham in Genesis to operate, buy and sale, do business and keep his family in the Egyptian System in Genesis 12:10

And there was a Famine (drought, no supplies, no open revelation) in the land, and Abraham went down to Egypt, to sojourn there. In Abraham's day, he abode under an Egyptian System, but as people of the 3rd Millennium we are not called to duplicate what the past fathers' did, we are called to not go down to Egypt. When you look in Genesis 26, Isaac was told not to go down to Egypt! Most of you when you hit a famine, you go back to pawning appliances, playing numbers, and worldly tactics instead of trusting in the divine flow for your life.

> *The universe wants to make you a millionaire but you keep trying to work in Egypt in a 9-5 job when there is a million dollar idea lying dormant in you.*

Prosperity is your heritage, it's your birthright. Get use to being rich, it's your calling in the earth.

And it came to pass the same day, Isaac servants came and told him, "We have founded Water! We have found life; abundances, prosperity and the well will not shut off!

Then Isaac sowed in that land in +verse 12 and received **in the SAME YEAR A HUNDREDFOLD, AND THE LORD BLESSED HIM! THE MAN WAXED GREAT AND WENT FORWARD, AND GREW UNTIL HE BECAME VERY GREAT! FOR HE HAD POSSESSION OF FLOCKS, HERDS, AND A GREAT STORE OF HERDMENS AND THE PHILISTINE ENVY HIM.**

Your enemies will increase when you prosper! People will not celebrate you when you walk in you millionaire status (all the father has ordained), but keep on walking into the overflow blessing, don't worry about the blessing blockers! Keep digging new wells!

Esek was the name of the first well, which meant coming in touch with substance, the first sign of prosperity, it was not the place of overflow, it was a place of expanding his mentality to release more abundances. The second well Isaac dug was called, Sitnah, which meant strife and contention, oppression, to try to maintain this well was to high maintenance. Isaac had to move on because the philistines tried to take this well, he released it and he dug the third well called Rehoboth, which meant a broad place, enlargement, greater expression, expansion unlimited.

The Philistine did not try to take this well, instead they wanted to make peace with Isaac. The fourth well was called Beersheba, meaning the well of fulfillment

Isaac went from the reality of being in a Famine, place of drought, place of want, place of lack developing a mentality attracting riches to become a Millionaire in the same year. Isaac continued to trust, Isaac defied the odds, and Isaac got the last laugh!

Your latter shall be greater than the former, but you can't quit! Keep the shovel in your hand.

So what if your business is not producing, so what if your bank account is low, keep digging within, keep the mindset of prosperity on, so if you want to get the same flow as prosperous Isaac, and then do what Isaac did, he obeyed God, sowed in the land he was assigned, and reap 100 fold the same year! God thru divine principles desire to take the famine out of your land, that you will come into the Anointing of Increase, where your wells will spring forth new prosperity to the level of a divine Overflow.

Millionaire Jacob

Genesis 28:16 - And Jacob awaked out of his sleep, and he said, surely the Lord is in this place, and I knew it not! Like Jacob you have to awake the Genius within you, the Magic in you has to be awakening for you to create abundances.

Jacob started out poor but ended up very rich. Jacob got definite about what he wanted. A double-minded man couldn't receive anything of the lord. Become single vision! Write down the details, color, amount, and be specific so your angels can bring it to pass.

Genesis 30:37-43 Jacob activated the Law of imaging. He took rods of green poplar, and hazel from the chestnut tree and pilled white strakes in them. He made the white appear in the rods. He set the rods that he pilled before the flocks in the gutters in the watering troughs so when the flocks came to drink, they should conceive. The flock conceived before the rods, and brought forth cattle ringstraked, speckled and spotted, and Jacob did separate the lambs and set the faces of the flocks toward the ringstraked, and all the brown in the flock of Laban, and he put his flocks by themselves, and put them not unto Laban's cattle. It came to pass, when so ever the stronger cattle conceived that Jacob laid the rods before the eyes of the cattle in the gutters, that they might conceive among the rods, but when the cattle were feeble, he put them not in, so that the feeble were Laban's and the stronger were Jacobs. Jacob the man increased exceedingly and had much cattle, maid servants, menservants, camels, and asses.

Millionaire Joseph

And there is not enough room to discuss Joseph. **Joseph dreamed** himself from the pit to the palace; Joseph went from sacks to wagonloads of money. Joseph was made the prime minister of the entire realm of Egypt.

Genesis 37:9 "and he dreamed yet another dream, and they hated him the more, for his dream, and for his words." It's never the so-called "devil" who steals your dream, it's those so-called relationships, kinfolks, cousins, and religious folks who are envious and jealous of seeing your dreams come to pass! You've got to get past all the negative, envy, jealous folks to fulfill your dream.

Millionaire Status Principle #40

Never let small minded people unbelief kill your dream.

God gave the dream seed of DOMINION to you! You have the entrepreneur spirit to dominate your domain, be fruitful, multiply, subdue and replenish the earth (4 laws of reproduction) forge ahead without petty indifference folk's opinions!

Genesis 39:2 And the lord was with Joseph and he was a prosperous man, and he was in the house of his master the Egyptian, and the master saw that the lord was with him, that the lord made all that he did prosper in his hand, and Joseph found favor in his sight, he served him, and he made him overseer over his house, he left all he had in Joseph's hand. *Genesis 41:37*

Joseph was president of then the wealthiest civilization of ancient times. Joseph had come into his millionaire status. Genesis 39:2 speaks that the lord was with Joseph and he became a prosperous man. One day Joseph was a forgotten slave, a convict, years later celebrated as the CFO of Egypt. King Pharaoh placed on Joseph the royal ring, a symbol of power and authority.

Be faithful in small tasks and God will reward you with larger responsibilities. Never seek power, seek responsibility, be a person who gets the job done on time and quickly! Get rid of excises. Consider the ant thy sluggard and be wise. There is no overnight success; success comes thru time and waiting for your season change. Celebrate and recognize when your season is, avoid attitudes when others are being celebrated. Every flower has a season to be planted, nurtured germinate and then it blossoms.

Joseph went from the pit to the palace!

Joseph was clothed in royal garments, a gold chain was placed around his neck, and he was made to ride in the second chariot behind the king of Egypt. Joseph had two sons, named Ephraim and Manasseh. Manasseh meaning "forgetting all the toil or God has made me to forget all my hardships."

His other son named Ephraim, meaning 'God has made me to be fruitful in the land of my affliction.' God will determine the place of your prosperity; sometimes it comes thru affliction. Stop running from the flames of adversity; adversity has an added benefit of blessings. Joseph had made the governor of Egypt, the riches of civilization in then the known world. Holdfast when your faith is a challenge, when your footing is unsure, the lord before the world has ordered your steps framed.

Even rose bushes have thorns on them; they still give a sweet fragrance in the midst of a test. You to will survive your season change and release a sweeter fragrance, the devil mean to kill you, but God has a hidden agenda.

The Divine has only one entry in the earth, thru the birth canal of all substance, man's unlimited imagination, unleashing millions of dreams from eternity to reality.

By implementing these principals of wealth, which begins by renewing the mind and grasping God's perspective and purpose for wealth, then you will see change in life.

Millionaire Status Principle #41
Your mind is the foundation and the manifestation of riches and wealth in your life. The mind of man is the mind of the master.

You have a mind that can create matter. Mind rules over matter. This is why Jesus could say, "Speak to the mountains." Most millionaires begin their quest with one creative ideal.

The creation process starts with a word, "in the beginning was the word". You are only 1 ideal, 1 relationship from landing your first Million dollars!

All things in the visible world originated from the spiritual realm. The

Manifestation process is first rehearsed in the psychic level of mind power. Mentally you must see, feel, taste and become the object you desire to manifest.

Most people have a negative programing when concerning wealth, money and relationships. You hear women and men who have been thru a bad relationship say, I will never marry again! So, the universe can not send the right soul mate, in the hard drive of consciousness is a negative prompter that must be removed. Many treat money the same way they treat relationships, they spend it, throw it away, squeeze it in church, never release it freely.

I tithe yet I am broke?? Do you release offerings at the same level? Are you still tipping God and expecting a Jabez experience?

Millionaire Status Principle #42

Practice law of Tithes/offerings

The most prominent millionaires of the world attribute their fortunes to tithing. The Colgate, Heinz, Kraft, J.C Penny, the famous Rockefeller's family, all used the royal law of 10%, the Tithed there way to riches.

The God system is Tithes & OFFERINGS. You are not a giver until you TITHE FIRST. Tithes opens the windows of divine overflow, your seed offerings determines how much flow through Tithe your time, time 10% of your day in meditating on God's principals.

Your offerings are the measurement which determines the degree of prosperity you will walk in! God will open your creativity up, then pour you out until there be not enough space to receive you, your business, your products will explode!

You can practice the Law of 10% and not receive until you remove the negative prompters from your mind, a poverty-stricken consciousness, an unforgiving thought toward your neighbor, resentment, anger, bitterness will block your wealth. Faith worketh by love.

You walk around with grudges, offenses toward people in your past, you talk and gossip about your leaders; you slander others, and are jealous of them, this is why your 10% is not working. You have to remove these negative demeaning thoughts out of your system.

God when he made you placed a million dollar ideal in you. Tap into the hidden resources of your mind. Stop allowing the world to pay for using your mind eight hours a day; use your own mind to create wealth for yourself. You came into the world equipped with an unlimited megabit mind, which has the answer to the manifestation and creation of all the countless dreams the father endowed within you. Sit in meditation; ask infinite wisdom to reveal the next enfoldment of your dreams, relationships career and perfect security for all realms of your life.

Wisdom is the thing princes and kings live by. Get wisdom, pursue wisdom and become a symbol of wisdom.

Market yourself, create your own products and utilize the internet to market, advertise and sale your dream. Form a mastermind group to realize each other's dreams. Stop waiting on a raise from your boss, become your own boss, give yourself a raise. Figure out how much you are worth and set out on a journey to discover your God gifts and realize your potential.

You become your most dominant thought! Rehearse your future daily thru meditation.

Sam Walton 1982-1992

The only member of this event ever to hula down wall street in a grass skirt-he did so after losing a bet to his employees that they couldn't raise their pretax profit above 8 percent-Walton was a small-time shopkeeper who invented the super-store as the most efficient way to serve rural communities. His stores profited not only by serving places that others overlooked but also by employing innovative inventory-control techniques, using computers to monitor all the stock everywhere, and making all the stores satellites of warehouses within a days drive. His shelves were never empty of anything for more then a few hours, he negotiated directly with manufacturers to keep his prices low, and he always took care of his employees-even if it meant dancing down wall street.

Warren Buffet 1930-

After learning at the knee of the Columbia Graduate School of Business Professor Benjamin Graham, the "Oracle of Omaha" scraped together a hundred thousand dollars to start an investment partnership when he was twenty-five, it had increased his clients' money by 30 percent a year when it was dissolved in 1969. Buffet then bought the small, worn-down textile firm Berkshire Hathaway, as a holding company it acquired under value companies whose stock values grew, and it is today a multibillion dollar power house that owns stock in the Washington Post, Coca-Cola, American Express, and Capitol Cities/ABC. Buffett retains a self-deprecating sense of humor and modesty: he does his own taxes, drives his own car, and says that Berkshire's stock is overvalued.

CHAPTER 6

Millionaire Shift to Kingdom

Every 40 years there is a season change, A Paradigm Shift. One season has to giveway to the next, the 3rd MILLENNIUM represents the season of Kings! We have witnessed the Protestant, the Pentecostal, and the Word of Faith, the Prophetic, and the Apostolic Movements and now the Era of Kings. Paradigm shift denotes a season of retraining and restructuring of the old, shifting to the new. New realities are being birthed, a complete new EPOCH!

Millionaire Status Principle #43
Recognize whose season it is, and what season you are in (winter, spring, summer or fall)!

(Prophetic word June 1, 2006).

This is the season I am initiating to inaugurate new Kings as establish authorities, without religion permission. Those who will understand there jurisdiction of Rule, raise up sons under authority to dominate the Regions, to fulfill the eternal purposes which I have ordered. They will trumpet the new sound, new tone in the earth. New paradigms, power bases in the earth are being instituted; teams of researchers, teams of strategists will come from the four winds of the earth. What ever you set your hand to do I will perform, teams of developers will purchase whole cities, creating new towns, Incorporated Governing Zion Cities.

Now we declare the Deborah, the Esther, the Solomon Anointing in the earth realm! Get ready for a take over of whole cities.

Millionaire's Taking Whole Cities

There must be a shifting in consciousness, a King consciousness to oversee cities.

St. Luke 19:17 "And he said unto him, well thou good servant, because you have been faithful in a very little, have authority over 10 cities!" Like wise he said to the other, have authority over 5 cities, while in meditation I receive their revelation of Kingship, the **father desire that you rule over cities.**

Imagination is creation, in Genesis 11:6 nothing was restrained from them which they have imagined! Get yourself in a consciousness where you deserve it, where you magnetize it, where you vibrate, radiate at the level of a Millionaire!

Develop A Rich Consciousness

Bill Gates who is a billionaire, CEO of Microsoft, became the richest man in the Universe, went from working at McDonald's to placing a dream seed to have a computer in every home in America! He imagined it, he dreamed it into being, he locked into purpose, and he developed the consciousness (mentality) of a King! (Entrepreneurs have a service consciousness while others have a work (9-5) consciousness?

Esther 4:13 "for if thou altogether boldest thy peace at this time, then shall there enlargement and deliverance arise to the Jews from another place, but thou and thy father's house shall be destroyed. And who knoweth whether thou art come to the kingdom for such a time as this?"

Such a time as this, we have never seen this time, but we have been assigned in this time; we are the answer for this generation. You have got to understand when God made you, he also made you divinely, uniquely original in his image predestined for a particular time in eternity. This is your time. You have been chosen for this generation! This is your season to face the challenges, find your calling, cause and be the Esther for your day. This time in the earth no one has seen. God is about to unleash 3rd millennium champions, 3rd millennium millionaires, and 3rd millennium prophets.

It's a time of great change, power shifting. We are in the midst of a technological revolution. We must pray that the spirit of Issachar be upon us, move from the deadness of tradition into the riches of kingdom. Esther rose for her generation. There must be a shifting in mentality, shifting in mindsets, in order to fulfill the mandate for our generation. We must move the church from a maintenance mentality to a mentality of managing the kingdom.

From Minister to Manager

Such a time as this, you are now being given a new direction, new identity, a fresh word has come from the throne, and there is no pattern to follow or copy. It's your season of change, fear not to cross over into kingdom riches. First become acquainted with wealth and riches. A poverty mentality will repel wealth, "poor-me" syndrome will cause money to flee from you; a Goodwill mentality will cause you never to walk in royalty, a Volkswagen mentality will cause you never to ride in a Mercedes. Get acquainted with wealth! Acquaint thyself now with the creator of the universe!

Your smile reflects kingdom, your dress radiates wealth, your walk demonstrates royalty and your integrity exemplifies royalty.

"When he showed the riches of his glorious kingdom and the honor of his excellent majesty many days, even hundred and fourscore days." Vashti the Queen made a feast for the women in the royal house that belonged to King Ahasuerus.

King Ahasuerus requested the presence of the Queen to come before his guests with the crown of royalty to show the people and the princes her beauty and her glory. God wants to display you to the world. He has ordained you to walk in riches wear royalty and display the riches of his kingdom.

But the Queen Vashti refused. Watch the spirit of Vashti, it will cause you to miss kingdom and abort God's rich destiny that you have been ordained to walk in. Queen Vashti refused to come to the next level. Therefore the King was very wroth, and his anger burned in him. God is divinely stripping his church, taking us through a process of cleansing, purging of tradition, and repositioning us into kingdom. There is a divine process of purging character, integrity, and reconstruction of dispositions, attitudes and moods before kingdom will be handed over to you.

God desires to give you a new heart! Queen Vashti refused, she failed to discern her season change and understand she was to represent the King not herself. The most important spirit we bring is obedience. She lost her place in the kingdom, lost her inheritance, lost her riches and royalties. Then God extended the scepter to a young unknown virgin named Esther. Esther submitted to the refining process, the grooming process, the purging and cleansing process.

Esther 1: 19 "if it please the king, let there be a royal commandment be written among the Persians, and the Medes, that it be not altered." That Queen Vashti comes no more before the King let the King give her royal estate to another. The Esther church is coming forth, a transfer of riches from the wicked to the righteous. God is sending you spiritual Mordecai's to groom, to purge, to purify and fit you in your royalty.

Now when every maids turn came to be in the presence of the King s chamber, after she had been purified for 12 moths, six months with precious oil, and six months with precious sweet odors. Now when the turn of Esther to appear before the king, the daughter of Abigail the uncle of Mordecai, who had taken her for his daughter, was come to go into the kings chamber, Esther obtained favor of all them that looked upon her. So Esther was taken into King Ahasuerus' royal house. And the King loved Esther above all women. She obtained grace and favor more then all the virgins, so he set the royal crown upon her head and made her Queen instead of Vashti.

Esther 5: 1 "Now it came to pass on the third day, Esther put on her royal apparel, stood in the inner court of the kings house, and the King sat upon his royal throne, in the royal house, and it was so when the King saw Esther the Queen standing in the court, that she obtained favor in his sight, and the King held out to Esther the golden scepter that was in his hand. Esther drew near, touched the top of the scepter, and the King said, what is thy Queen Esther request?"

Millionaire Status Principle #44

You don't have to necessarily like the person who is occupying the throne, but your faithfulness to the King determines the jurisdiction of your rule. In leadership, there is the changing of the guard, the passing of patons to the next generation. The patons is never passing to a spectator in the crowd, the paton is passed to the one who takes on the spirit of his leader.

Elijah said if you see me, you shall receive a double portion of my spirit, if you become one with me!

Wisdom Cometh!

Proverbs 4:7 "Admonish us to get wisdom. Wisdom is the principal thing, or it's the thing princes live by, therefore get wisdom, but in all thy getting get understanding." The three cornerstones of life are wisdom, understanding and knowledge. Knowledge is the gathering of facts, understanding is the interpretation of facts, but wisdom is the application of facts.

It's imperative we establish wisdom schools in society. The ancient Hebrews youth were reared in wisdom. Many people have college degrees, come into some type of fame, but they lack the wisdom of God. Many have children out of wedlock, in jail, serving the world's God in a financial ruckus and rebelling against the God of the universe.

Get wisdom before you go to war; seek out counsel with the wise before you lunch into the deep. To be successful establish at least five mentors who are at least highly successful in the field of your endeavor. Ask for divine skill and divine intelligence of the Holy Spirit to release upon all projects. Wisdom has to be demonstrated to our youth thru the actions of their leaders. Solomon didn't ask God for big wheels, new tennis shoes, a house on the hill or the fame of the world. Solomon asked God for wisdom.

Wisdom cometh! Wisdom cometh! Wisdom cometh in all realms of our life! Infinite divine skillful wisdom cometh! We need to balance all revelation with solid truth. Most people need to ask wisdom cometh instead money cometh? Lord teaches me to manage what I have, teach me to stick with a budget, teach me to not be an impulsive buyer, teach me not to go buy groceries hungry. Teach me to save, to invest my money. Wisdom cometh!

Princes live by wisdom. Wisdom causes you to see in dark places, wisdom unlocks the mysteries of life, wisdom transfers into wealth, wisdom makes your name great, wisdom causes you to inherit the throne of glory.

In the beginning you were umbilically tied to the creator of the universe. You are composed of the same substance that created the world. Express your creative abilities.

Father, we ask that you release light, divine supernatural supreme wisdom, skills and intelligence to all realms of my life. That I be the essence of Christ, the epitome of success and that my borders will be enlarged, my world would expand and the kingdom be demonstrated thru my integrity and lifestyle. That I surround myself with wise counselors whom will assist me to come into the fullness of Christ and experience him in his length, the height, the breath and depths of my being. Allow the creativity of the Holy Spirit to explode within me, releasing moneymaking ideals, my creative mind is creating as a creator. I am a money magnet, I attract new customers to my business. I radiate wealth, and wealth is my birthright!

The Power of Money

The bible speaks where there's a vision the people flourish, where there's not a vision the people perish. The other side of the coin is without money there is no people or vision! Money attracts people. To get the attention of the masses we have to generate wealth.

Money is a medium of exchange. Stop complaining about not having money. What service, what product, and what gift are you giving in exchange for money?

Money is a symbol of freedom, beauty, luxury, power, refinement, and rich living.

It's takes money to keep churches, business and family striving. It takes nothing to maintain a surviving church or business. God desires that you be striving with wealth and not surviving until the next payday or offerings. Money gives us the authority in the earth to rule as kings. We have spiritual authority, but in order to buy up our entire block, we need to come into wealth. Money answers all things.

Millionaire's bounce back

Most of us have made mistakes in our past regarding money and business due to the ignorance of our religious upbringings. So don't allow that ignorance to steal from your future because you made bad decisions in the past. Most millionaires have lost all their wealth 2 to 3 times bounced back and changed the world.

Some environments perpetuated poverty, which has caused a lot of heartaches, divorces, crime, pain and misery. Some people were raised with a slave mentality, "poor me" syndrome and barely get by mentally.

Now, its time to walk out of your past, out of tradition, and away from the curse. Release your cultural religious pride; renew your mind to the gospel of the kingdom, a covenant filled with blessings regardless of your race.

Once you cut covenant with Jehovah—God, all which belong to God then belongs to you, all that is becomes yours. You become joint-heir to the throne, you become an heir to God, and you are no longer alienated from the covenant. You then can decree a thing and it can be established.

You are then a citizen of a royal rich kingdom. Renew your mind; the blessings of the lord are yea and amen in him! God is about to restore your name, your credit and all the years where the locust devoured you thru ignorance of your covenant rights to prosper and be the head and not the tail.

Ex: 12:35 "and the children of Israel did according to the word of Moses, and borrowed of the Egyptians jewels of silver, and jewels of gold, and raiment's."

Gen 24-32, "and the lord hath blessed my master greatly, and he is become great, and the lord has given him flocks, and herds, and silver, and gold, and menservants and maidservants and asses."

Due 8:18, but thou shalt remember the lord thy God, it is he who giveth thee the power to get wealth to establish his covenant upon the earth.

Ps35:27, the lord have pleasure in the prosperity of his saints . . .

Matt 17: 27 "notwithstanding, lest we should offend them, go thou to the sea, cast in a hook, and taketh up the fish that first cometh up, and when thou hast opened his mouth, thou shalt find a piece of money, that take to give unto them for me."

Ecc10: 19 "money answereth all things!"

The Bible has a lot to say in regards to money and prosperity. We want to silence all the religious zealots who have taken a vow of poverty. God desires to have all your bills paid. God desires to have you debt free. God desires you live on 90%. Stir up your gift of money! If you are in bondage, in debt, in lack, how can you be a witness to the world, when they represent the rich and the famous?

This poverty mentality came from the spirit of religious error and the tradition of man. We must minister in the spirit of truth and conduct business in the spirit of truth. Money is a medium of exchange; money was placed in the earth as ideals. Money chases ideals, when one desires more money, one need's creative ideals. God is not first of all concerned about how much money you have. You determine your value on the earth. The question is how much do you think you are worth?

Money purpose

Money is attracted to you, your business at the level of an expert service, skill, abilities, loyalty, wisdom, and excellence of character, communication and the development of solid proven relationships of those involved. (Law of attraction) relationships have to pass the test of time and pressure, even in business.

Biblically the sole purpose of money is to establish the covenant of God on the earth. We have to renew our minds in regards to prosperity and accumulating money. God is also a God of cash. The world system is to get you to buy on time, but most don't pay on time, which equals bondage and high interest.

If you put away $100.00 monthly at 17 years old in an IRA retirement account then by the age of 60, you would have at least $250,000.00. The American system programs youth and adults to spend money instead of investing in themselves and the kingdom.

God desires you to prosper! God desires you to become the word manifested in the flesh! You have to make a decision to prosper. Indecision and procrastination is a thief of time. You have to directly interrupt the cycle of debt and poverty. Plan to be rich, associate with other wealthy people, create a mentality of wealth, think wealth thoughts and get out of poverty teaching churches.

You do not have to carry on a legacy of debt and poverty from your former generation. There is a changing of the guard, changing of administration, it's a new day. Moses is dead, its Joshua day. Thinking is different, administration is different, and concepts, ideals, and anointing are designed to usher in an economic revival of wealth!

The law is perfect

Joshua 1:8 "This book of the law shalt not depart from your mouth, but thou shalt meditate therein day and night, that thou mayest observe to do all that is written therein. Then thou shalt make thou way prosper and make good success. Thou shall meditate on the desired results." You have to get into a medicated state. Paint rich, vivid, pictures in the corridor of your mind to birth your reality. Hear the sound of riches, prosperity, wealth and health around you as you meditate. Think on rich things for others. Meditation is medicine for your soul. As a man thinketh in his heart so is his reality. Get into the state, or mentality of what you want to bring forth. Resist fear, worry and doubt. It's the father's good pleasure to give you the kingdom. Your own thoughts will produce a rich prosperous reality or it will produce a poverty reality. Jesus said a good man would bring forth-good things out of the treasures of his heart!

Meditate on the desired results.

Millionaire Summary

1. Have a burning desire! Start your success program today, don't procrastinate.
2. Write out your specific wealth goals.
3. Increase the value of yourself. Use the other 95% of your brainpower.
4. Don't underestimate your abilities.
5. See yourself, being, doing, and having the exact images in your mind.
6. Impress rich pictures in your consciousness.
7. Believe you can come into "millionaire status" package your dream.
8. Set your sail to accomplish your dream.
9. Speak, think, feel, and vibrate wealth.
10. Avoid negative, demeaning, descending attitudes & people.

CHAPTER 7

Millionaire Kings Movement!

The 3rd millennium church will have a new design.

You will witness churches and businesses moving into the Kingdom, establishing gymnasiums, aquatic pools, large weight rooms, movie theatres, shopping malls and restaurants, to meet the needs of the whole man. The storefront mentality cannot meet the needs of the whole family. This will enable the world to transfer wealth back to the church on Monday. You were destined and ordained to walk in wealth

Movement of Kings Consciousness Global TAKEOVER!

Daniel 6:1-4 Kings!

The church in the earth is moving beyond the 5 fold ministry of the apostle, prophet, evangelist, pastor/teacher, this is the age God is preparing kings in the earth, whole regions will change by the wealth and authority of these new kings, whole cities, states, and nations will be effected by these governing anointing which will bring economics to the nations. That's why many of you that are reading this book have been going thru crazy trials, you don't fit in tradition, God had changed your message, taking you to a different level, you are apart of the new anointed generation of kings of the earth.

Daniel 12:21 and he changed the times and the seasons, he removed the kings and set up the kings given! He gave wisdom unto the wise and knowledgeable to them that knows understandings.

Kingdom Mandate

Each generation since Adam was given a Mandate of Dominion, to walk in obedience to the covenants and expand thru family unity to church, to community, to city, to state and then to national affluence. Man's **agenda** is to destroy and abort your destiny, family, and breed disunity in the church, cause rebellion in youth, pervert the purpose of men, and curse the human family.

Each generation starts with one gene. God genetically designed us in his image with his genes. You are not here by accident, neither coincident, you are here by ordination by God, predestined before the foundation of the earth. You were programmed, and given a divine assignment, that is why you have been going thru so much hell. People will attack you to stop your assignment.

You have an assignment to change the world! We can't peacefully coexist with an enemy. We are here to take over. Our assignment is to finish the unfinished works of Christ, unfinished Business. Our assignment is to create wealth to leave a legacy that our children's children will not have a care in the world. One of my assignments is to travel the earth impart a fresh revelation to not only destroy the generational curses but build generational wealth.

Roman 1:11 for I long to see you that I may impart to you some spiritual gift to the end you may be established.

11 Chronicles 20:20, believe in the Lord your God, so shall ye be establish, believe his prophets so shall ye prosper!

The church must begin to build warrior priests, warrior believers and warrior kings who will take their rightful place in the earth. The church and the earth are in a season change. It's a time of prophetic realignments, reassessments of church visions, retaining of leadership, and evaluating past errors to avoid a transfer of religious error. We can have good intentions but still minister in error; there is truth, and the spirit of error.

DEBT IS a virus on your mental computer that's producing the same cycle of your past which is causing a curse. The cures for debt are practicing Kingdom principles and activate the laws of seedtime and harvest. You will notice in the absence of money, there are more depression, sickness, divorce and crime. Most family, marital, relationship and church problems deal with the lack of money or the abundance of money. God must become you source, not money, individual consciousness must be awaken to the abundances in the universe.

What is debt? **Debt is a condition of owing, an obligation or liability to another. Develop a cash flow!** When you worship God with your money, give a sacrifice to your church, release your covenant tithes, then you enter into a life of blessings Deuteronomy 7:28.

God is returning the true father mentality to the church that will not prostitute the people of their tithes and offerings but fulfill their vision and teach wisdom principles to a people who will manifest true riches.

Millionaire Status Principle #45

Find your five expert mentors and become one with them.

We are called to relieve the oppressed, set the captives free and preach the gospel without cost to the lost. We have to destroy this storefront mentality from the church; small minds cannot fulfill large dreams. This progressive revelation will cause many to examine their callings, visions and long-term goals.

Money is the worlds God, our primary role is to dethrone the worlds God and make the worlds God our servant to establish the rule of the king.

Money must become your servant and not your boss. Many people in the pews want to move in their anointing, what we need in spirit of wisdom and obedience. Help finance the vision of your house!

First Fruits

Tithe to your church, give large offerings. God desires to take over the earth! Stop tipping God! Honor the lord with your first fruits; honor God with the first of all your increase.

Tithing is your investment in God's economic system to take the world!

There are some preordained blessings, predetermined blessings IN STORE FOR YOU. Don't let your adversary cause you to eat your first fruit tithes and offerings. People will cause you to eat your seed and destroy your harvest. Activate **the law** of **Circulation,** money is currency, a current flows, **money must circulate.** Lack comes due to breaking the law of circulation. Give all and it shall be given unto you, good measure, press down, shaken together, running over shall men give circulate back to you. Keep the first fruit holy before the Lord, worship God with the first fruits, then God will pour you out blessings where there is not room to receive.

Some theologians are releasing error to the body of Christ, telling them they don't have to tithe, that this was old covenant. The old points to the new, Jesus was our first-fruit, and he made the lump holy. Thru God giving his first born we are redeemed from the curse of sin, sickness and the second death. When you release your first fruits you are redeemed from debt, from repossession, from bankruptcy, from the cycle of poverty. Interrupt the cycle of poverty today! Tithe from your business income, sow crazy seeds into the kingdom, and reap crazy blessings.

PR.3:9 honor the Lord with thy first fruits of all thy increase.

EX22: 29 Thou shall not DELAY to give thy first fruits of thy ripe fruit.

Lev.2: 12 as for thy first fruits, ye shall offer it to the Lord.

St. John 10: 10 the thief cometh not to steal, kill and to destroy, I come that ye would have life, and life more abundantly. When you activate kingdom principles of offering your first fruits then the devil is upset with you. Your adversary wants to kill your harvest by taking your first fruit seed. Give the seed, and reap the harvest. It's a law of seedtime and harvest. And if you have eaten your seed, redeem yourself!

Lev27:31 and if a man will redeem ought of his tithes, he shall add a fifth part thereof. That is multiply what you ate by five and adds the amount to the original 10% and releases that to your storehouse.

Genesis 8:22 while the earth remained, seedtime and harvest, cold and winter, day and night shall not cease.

There should be millionaires in the church. Youths need to learn about stocks and bond, mutual funds, **investing in** IRA **accounts,** and understand real estate and insurance.

Economic Keys to Increase Wealth

Millionaire Summary

- Create a wealth building club
- Read daily the Millionaire Status, share with a friend.
- Read Money, Fortune 500, Entrepreneur, Success, Franchises &

Business Magazines

- Study the stock market, learn about mutual funds,
- Open an IRA account at an early age
- Pay your creditors on time
- Develop a vehicle to have a positive cash flow, purpose to own a Franchise.
- Get a second job, Work is not a curse!
- Start a family business
- Make ten new friends outside of your regular comfort zone monthly, keep a list of new friends, and cultivate old relationships.

Russell Sage 1816-1906

He seems to have become one of the wealthiest people in American history simply by being in the right place at the right time. His early investments made him comfortable, but a chance meeting with the roundly despised Jay Gould made him rich beyond his dreams. Gould became his friend and ally, and under Gould's aegis he made a fortune in the stock market, where he is credited with originating puts and calls. He preferred small returns to big risks, and he eventually turned to money lending; at one time he was purported to have twenty-seven million dollars out on loan. Luck was apparently ever on his side; he survived an assassin's bomb that killed his clerk and the assassin and died quietly at home.

THE UNITED STATES OF AMERICA
FEDERAL RESERVE NOTE
THIS NOTE IS LEGAL TENDER FOR ALL DEBTS, PUBLIC AND PRIVATE
G 05555555 A
WASHINGTON, D.C.
ONE HUNDRED DOLLARS
100

CHAPTER 8

Millionaire Power Shifting In the New Millennium

From Entre*poor*neur to Entrepreneur!

Economics has been the buzzword for the 21st century. During the last election, the President's focus was on stabilizing the nation with a new economy. The prophetic parallel word for the ambassadors of the kingdom is also spiritual economics. God is not just concerned about you getting saved; he is concerned about NATION TAKING! In order to experience the invisible kingdom in all realms of your life, you must have a power shift from the old traditional paradigm to the new paradigm of kingdom.

Entrepreneurs take action on their dreams; entrepoorneur remains poor because they listen to everyone's opinion about their genius ideal!

Millionaire Status Principle #46

There must be a shifting from the old mindset to the new mindset; insanity is doing the same thing over and over again receiving the same results. There has to be an assessment of strategic plans, long term effectiveness and a mastermind group to ensure success.

Whole companies have gone into bankruptcy. Many large corporations have created mergers to stabilize their own economy and maintain leverage to avoid hi-layoffs and down sizing. In the new millennium it will be imperative for businesses to merge in order to survive a fast changing society.

The competitive edge from the business secular world is not to exist in the sacred world. We are called to complete and not compete. There must be a restructuring of leadership and a retraining of management. A sovereign person, a sovereign_nation is not defined, confined or controlled by anyone.

Mike Connaway, renown author of the book, *Sabotage*, says "It's impossible to go to the Next level if you are not a sovereign, free individual." This means to be self-govern and for you take back control of your destiny. You decide where you live, where you work, what you drive, and you become an independent thinker.

> *99% of Millionaires are Sovereign persons, high performers, self govern, and independent thinkers of a system! They create NEW PARADIGMS! They are NOT bound to a religious system or living under an American Nightmare. They are Creators, producers and manufacture ideals from their own MIND!*

Our nation is 7 trillion dollars in debt. We are sending major business out of the USA. The rich keep getting richer, there is no middle class and the poor keep getting poorer. When there is a decrease in employment, crime and domestic violence increase. People get desperate and seek out psychics, play numbers, bingo and lottery games out of fear and they lack prophetic insight in the church. But God is raising up a company of prophets who will prophesy to the winds and bring restoration of kingdom.

Recently Boeing in Seattle Washington moved to the city of Chicago. Many families were left in the dark; the governor of Washington State was in a panic and couldn't compete with such swift changes of big business. The Seattle economy lost millions of dollars. Seattle became dependant on the longevity of the Boeing enterprises. Prophetically God is speaking to the believers as well as the church. These are definite signs of the times. There is a constant downsizing of large business, and now is the time **to position yourself where you can have the greatest leverage** to be ready for a TRANSFER OF WEALTH.

In the coming new millennium we will experience a changing economy. The forecast is dim for many markets and businesses that do not change but were key players in the past century. Inflation has placed many booming businesses of the past century out of business. Leaders must stay abreast to change and incorporate fresh innovative ideals to compete with fast changing society.

> *Correction flows from the top down, not from the bottom up, correction is not rejection.*

Age of Hi-Tech

This is a High-tech age, robotics, computer technology, communications, scientists are cloning satellites that are being placed on mars, and graphic designs are changing so swift that electronics systems can't keep up with the pace.

Systems of education, schools, business, political systems, religious systems, and economic systems, have controlled society. The current has produced a 20/80 problem, resulting in the masses being controlled by a herd mentality. The 20% (producers) are taking care of the 80% (consumers) because the system has produced entrepoorneurs instead of entrepreneurs.

The World's system should no longer dictate the destiny of people. The power shift is to change the current system to 80/20 (80% producers/20% consumers) to create capital and a self sustaining economy. There is a divine call of KINGDOM.

Computer systems must be used in the church and schools to keep abreast with the fast changes in today's economic system. Emerging leaders must become economic strategists, computer literate, direct large scales of operations and reach into the global world with every tool God has given them.

Economic strategies and the science of developing systems and management must be taught to the advantage of positioning the non-profit and for profit businesses to be highly sophisticated and effective to even compete with the global world leaders such as OPEC (Organizing of Petroleum Exporting Counties) and APEC (Asian Pacific Economic Council) nations in taking and determining the destiny of the World Nations.

Management teams must address housing and population transience, health measures and health care needs; start hospitals, convalescent centers, study the crime statistics of a region, and immigration pattern and become bilingual in diverse language.

We have to position ourselves to be invited at the tables of those who rule the nations. We must address the nation problems and no longer be considered to be insignificant.

Money in the earth represents authority! By massing wealth, we will be invited to the councils of the global world who determine the policies and prosperity of the whole nations. Prophetically, God is repositioning ministries and placing key leaders in strategic locations that will determine the destiny of nations and rule in righteousness.

In **a season of change, it demands an adjustment of attitudes and shifting of mindsets to be prepared for the coming new season.**

Become self-sufficient; develop a cash flow vehicle to ride you into your first million.

Many churches have become lethargic with rituals, ceremonies, songs and programs while other nations are buying up the very property in which they sit on. There has been a definite power shift in our economy and in the world's largest nation. The church cannot stand and continue business as usual. The church must produce its own capital and adopt a new economic policy to become self govern to expand to every nation with economic power. In a recent article in Black Enterprise Magazine, September 2006 article commented on the much needed paradigm shift of the church, from a storefront mentality to creating financial infrastructure to be self govern. The questions asked: "How many mega churches have become owners of banks, life insurance companies, credit unions, or savings and loan organizations? The spending power has not change. *When we examine the statistical analysis of church finances globally, we find churches have become a high risk to community banking institutions. Banks seldom loan money to churches, and therefore the church must* ***develop its own Economy, to ensure the vision will survive all season changes. The church must have its own systems of education, financial, health, and insurance.***

> *You will witness a power shift toward the 3rd millennium, the church that moves beyond tradition, accumulates wealth and increase capital will rule in the next millennium.*

Joshua, Moses is dead, now arise and take this people over Jordan! A New season demands new administration. As we discuss Moses, we are not looking primarily at a man.

Moses is a mindset. The Joshua generation had a different spirit, different mindset, different agenda, different administration and a different song than Moses people. Moses people were full of rebellion.

You cannot put new wine in old wineskins!

Daniel 2:21" and he changes the times and the seasons: he removed kings and setteth up new kings. Giveth wisdom to the wise, and knowledge to them that know understanding."

Job 22:24, "then shalt thou lay up gold as dust and the gold of ophir as the etones of the brooks."

Hagg 2:12 "the glory of the latter house shall be greater than the glory of the former house and in these house shall be prosperity!"

Isaiah 45:2-3, "I ***will go before you,*** *and make the crooked places straight, I will break in pieces the gates of brass, and cut in sunder the bars of iron: and I will give thee the treasures of darkness, and* ***the hidden riches of secret places,*** *that thou mayest know that I, the Lord, which call thy by thy name, am the God of Israel."*

Discipline The Rich Feed The Poor!

This war we are in is for world domination, taking territory and not a Sunday morning thing. True bishops are called to officiate events, which will affect the world and inaugurate the reception of Jesus Christ. The church should own up franchises, shopping malls, grocery stores, movie theatres, and banks. King Solomon gave away cities.

Start out in life to market your gifts to every soul on the planet, not get a JOB. Never pursue money, create a skill, develop a service to serve the community, write a book, sing a song, and discover your gift then money will pursue you! Money chases ideas!

Father in the name of Jesus, I ask for divine supreme wisdom, divine intelligence and skill is released. That creative ideals would flow through my spirit causing **money-making ideals** to come unto me, allow me to find "the fish with the coin in his mouth", to cause me to come into the perfect career, business in which you ordained for my life before the world was formed in order for me to experience salvation in all realms of my life.

What is wealth? Wealth is the state of having money or property and a great amount of worldly possession. Wealth is affluence. It has the power to influence change. Wealth is also having economic value. What is wealth for? The wealth is to establish the covenant of prosperity in the earth, the wealth is to destroy the poverty mentality and destroy a mentality that has created a generation of beggars. Debt represents an absent of wisdom and knowledge of how to accumulate wealth and a violation of the covenant of God.

When one walks in obedience to the covenant, you can expect miracles. When one walks out from obedience you will experience disaster.

Proverbs 26:2, "The curse causeless shall not come, or the curse doesn't come without a cause!" Credit cards, high -interest items, I got to have it now mentality are a few reasons many are in the debt bondage.

Millionaire Summary

1. Honor the Lord with your first fruits, tithes and offerings to your storehouse.
2. Finish High School and go to College.
3. Get a career and build a solid savings account over time.
4. Invest in an IRA, (individual retirement account) early.
5. Open your own business; work hard beyond 8 to 5pm.
6. Purchase items with cash.
7. Start a wealth building club. Start today! Dream again! Unlock someone else dreams. Whose dreams are you unlocking?
8. Find 5 mentors to speak wisdom into your life!

Henry Ford 1863-1947

The son of Angelo-Irish immigrants, Ford began an automobile while employed as a machinist for the Edison Illuminating Company in Detroit; he represented his Quadricycle in 1896. In 1901 he entered a racer of his own design in a ten mile match race and won, then he persuaded an investor to back the formation of the Ford Motor Company in 1903. In 1908 he introduced the sturdy and affordable model T, and he constantly lowered its price, from $850 in 1908 down to $290 by the mid twenties, believing that greater volume would make up for the lower profit margin. He was right: By 1914 the company was selling 248,000 Model T's a year, capturing close to 50 percent of the market. But he kept it in production far too long, nearly sinking the company before switching to the Model A in 1927.

Andrew W. Mellon 1855-1937 & Richard B. Mellon 1858-1933

When he was nineteen, Andrew joined his father's bank, T. Mellon & Sons; his younger brother Richard came aboard as partner after their father's retirement in 1886. Thanks to their complimentary personalities, they joined a warm-and effective-family and business partnership. Andrew managed the books while Richard met with customers. Pittsburgh, where they did business, was the center of booming coal, steel, oil, and railroad industries. They had a keen eye for promising business ventures and backed a number of companies that became industrial giants, among them the Aluminum Company of America, Gulf oil, and Union Steel. In 1921 President Harding appointed Andrew Secretary of the Treasury; his eleven-year tenure brought about a dramatic reduction in the national debt. In 1937 Andrew donated his impressive art collection, plus money for a building to house it, to create the National Gallery of Art. Richard's passion was reviving rundown Pittsburgh.

Peter A. Widener 1834-1915

A groundbreaker of nineteenth-century consolidation, he knotted together all the street railways in Philadelphia and then helped assemble American Tobacco, U.S. Steel, and the International Mercantile Marine Company. He held his first job in a meat shop, won a contract to supply mutton to all the Civil War troops within ten miles of Philadelphia, and invested his fifty-thousand-dollar profit, plus money he earned holding local political offices, in street railways and Philadelphia traction companies. Under his eye, Philadelphia streetcar technology advanced from horse to cable to electric, and his money and expertise helped build lines in New York and Chicago as well.

Nicholas Longworth 1782-1863

Patriots confiscated all the property belonging to his loyalist family during the American Revolution, and perhaps that goaded him to set out to make his millions in land trade. Starting out in law, he traded his very first fee- two second hand copper steels- for thirty-three acres of land later worth $2 million. He then bought his boss's cow pasture for $5,000; its worth grew to $1.5 million under his ownership. His real estate deals brought him great wealth, but he carved a more lasting mark as a leader in strawberry and black raspberry to America, and his experiments greatly boosted this nation's fruit production.

THE UNITED STATES OF AMERICA
FEDERAL RESERVE NOTE
ONE HUNDRED DOLLARS
THIS NOTE IS LEGAL TENDER FOR ALL DEBTS, PUBLIC AND PRIVATE
G 05555555 A
WASHINGTON, D.C.
100

CHAPTER 9

Millionaire Activation

Did you not know there are spiritual laws of the universe that will guarantee wealth? The only different of a poor person and a rich person is that they operate under different laws.

The same as there are laws of gravity, laws that governs electricity. Operate and activate these laws, you can claim your rich inheritance. Millionaire ideals that will produce wealth have to be activated. God's desire is to bring you into a wealthy place, Psalm 66:12. You have to learn the laws that govern the universe, whether you are a child of God or not, the laws work. The law is perfect. Whether you believe in the law of gravity or not nothing is going to save you if you fall off a tall building.

If you are ignorant of these laws you will remain poor, you will die poor, and your grandchildren will have to take care of your funeral arrangements. There is the law of rest; break this law and you will lose your health, ask any overworked, underpaid friends. The hospital is full of people who violate the law of rest. Activate these laws and begin to prosper. Begin today!

God placed laws to govern the universe that has nothing to do with your religious affiliation, your race, or your belief system. Your belief system is the thermostat that determines your universal destiny. Whether your church teaches these laws will not put them into effect. Hosea 4:6, "My people are destroyed due to lack of knowledge."

There is the entrance of knowledge, and then there is progressive knowledge. There is light and then there is clear light. Wisdom and light comes in degrees. The light of the fifties cannot sustain us in the new millennium; you have to follow the glory cloud. The glory that you are flowing in now is not all the glory of God. There is within you an unrevealed or unveiled glory.

No one can contain the full glory of God, therefore, God gives us a glimpse, rays, realms and degrees of glory. God desires you go from one glory to another. To enter into a new glory, means there must be a shifting of mind sets. Prophets of the new millennium will bring fresh revelation to the earth to launch you into a brand new season of prosperity and increase Jesus said "the kingdom is within you!" See all your dreams become a reality.

Joshua 1:8 "The book of the law shall not depart out of thy mouth; but thou shall meditate there in day and night, that thou may observe and do all that is written there in, then thou shall make thy way prosperous and have good success."

Begin today to activate the laws that govern the kingdom of God. The law of love, the law of increase, the law of tithing, the law of business, the law of prosperity, law of faith, law of sowing and reaping and the law of dominion. These supernatural laws supersede the natural laws.

Now go forth, manifest and demonstrate the riches and glories of the royalty of the kingdom within. Open up your creative intelligence mind, tap into the hidden resources and the endless astronomical, infinite, God endowed abilities within you. Have a burning desire to excel in life, use kingdom laws and principles, and avoid get-rich quick schemes.

Don't allow tradition to handicap your imagination. **Thomas Edison dreamed** of a lamp that could be operated by electricity, began where he stood to put his dream into action, despite more than ten thousand failures, he stood by his dream, travailed until it became a reality. George Washington carver discovered 100 products from the simplicity of a peanut.

The **Wright Brothers dreamed** of a machine that would fly thru the air, they were called crazy. Today we fly in jets that can cross the earth in lighting speed. **Marconi dreamed** of a system for harnessing the intangible forces of the ethers. It may be interesting to know that Marconi's friends had taken him into custody, to examine him in a psychiatric hospital. **Einstein**, who discovered the theory of relativity, his elementary teacher told him he was retarded but he ended up splitting molecules and atoms.

John Bryant wrote the pilgrim progress, finest of English literature. **Colonel Sanders** end up at the age of 51 with only his Social Security check of about $192.00, knocked on 999 doors receiving a "no" answer for his chicken recipe, in spite of the odds continued, persevered and today there are over 100,000 stores in over 50 nations. **Benjamin Banneker** created an almanac, **Alexander Miles** invented the elevator, and **Charles Drew** found the blood plasma, in spite of all odds.

Abraham Lincoln ran for president over 4 times and lost, but he never lost sight of his dream, and refused to live a life of mediocrity. When elected he freed the slaves with his emancipation proclamation speech. David faced Goliath; Joshua fought the battle of Jericho. Moses started with a speech impediment and later led over 600,000 people out of bondage. You use stumbling blocks as stepping stones, use your obstacles as opportunities, maximize your gifts, and utilize your talents. Dare to be different. Be a burning bush for your generation! Turn all your tragedies into triumphs. There is a greater wisdom within you that even Aristotle and Socrates didn't tap into. What lies within you is more powerful than what lies behind you, forward ever, backward never!

Helen Keller born deaf and later blind disciplined her life and defied all odds. Beethoven, an expert musician was deaf and he performed for Mozart. **Milton was blind**; he became one of the greatest composers of our time. You now have the golden opportunity to package your dreams, develop your skills, market your abilities and economically empower yourself. Dare to discipline yourself! Impress your subconscious with rich thoughts, rich pictures and rich sounds and see the manifestation of your visions.

Jesus Christ told his disciples, "I will destroy this body but in three days I will raise it up." He defied nature, resurrected the third day, and appeared unto them, descended into the heavens, he dared to be different! Now is your chance to leave your footprints in the sand. Go ahead dream again; realize the millionaire possibilities in you.

Now you see from the father's perspective, nothing can stop you; you are a miracle on the way to happen. You are on the journey of discovery, go forth, and take the chains of limitations, the chains of doubts, and the invisible chains of fear off. Dare to dream big dreams! Turn all your obstacles into opportunities. Become the word manifested and demonstrated in the flesh. Soar as the one whose image you were made in. You were created to do an exploit in life, you were engineered for success, you were designed to experience the best in life, and you are God's rich child of the loving universe. Come to the place where your incredible dreams and impossibilities become manifested blessings. Now go! Make your impossible dreams a reality, shape your own destiny, and began today . . . Know that the force is with you, angels are waiting on your word to take you to the next level. **'Cogito ergo sum' I think therefore I am!**

Declaration of Financial Empowerment

From this day forward, I declare my vigilant and lifelong commitment to financial empowerment. I pledge the following:

1. Use homeownership to build wealth
2. Save and invest 10% to 15% of my after-tax income
3. Commit to a program of retirement planning and investment

4. Engage in sound budget, credit, and tax management practices
5. Measure my personal wealth by net worth, not income
6. Be proactive and knowledgeable about investing, money management, and consumer issues
7. Provide access to programs that will educate my children about business and finance
8. Support the creation and growth of profitable, competitive black-owned enterprises
9. Use a portion of my wealth to strengthen my community
10. Ensure that my wealth is passed on to future generations

Millionaire Vibrations

Millionaire Ideals which will produce millionaire lifestyles have to be activated! The atmosphere of creativity to release genius powers have to be created in the home to create young millionaires, both partners must work in unison to set the correct environment to produce maximum effective child geniuses.

It's a known fact that in music, a certain note or sound of an opera singer can break glass? Sounds, vibrations and positive energy will magnetize prosperity and abundance but the wrong energy, sound will release poverty and chaos.

Example, Jimmie Hendrix would play one cord on his guitar at concerts and people would begin to act in unseemly ways because the medulla, a mechanism of the brain, releases certain chemicals according to sounds, vibrations and tones. Sounds of Hip Hop, sounds of Symphony music, sounds of Jazz, all produce different effects on people that is why, in the Bible, Elijah said, "Bring me a minstrel!"

Sounds have waves, waves produce energy, energy releases notes to your syntax that control all functions and signals of the mind. This is why certain children make A's in school, while others make F's. What type of sounds, pitches, and tones of greatness are they hearing in your home?

Movie Theater's & highly sophisticated business corporations play subliminal mind altering music while employees work to maximize productivity in the work environment. The subliminal music is below the threshold of conscious perception, subliminal messages to produce a desired result. There is subliminal music to produce prosperity, success, relaxation, relief of stress, to lose weight and to magnetize money.

Faith is the sound of things hoped for, the note of things not realized.

Prophetically God is shifting you to a higher realm of revelation, to a place where you can't even imagine, where money is like dust in the air. The major problem is God convincing you to shift to a higher imagination of self so you can manifest at the degree of revelation knowledge, magnetizing rich energy and creating the vacuum to attract the ideal lifestyle.

Key is to spend more time mediating and not mediworrying! Start broadcasting what you desire, you shall decree, it shall be establish! God will bring you from the gutter most to the uttermost, from a beggar to a King!

Seems like things around you are breaking down, its time to SHIFT to A higher realm in the level of prosperity and wealth to come into your first million dollar.

Master Key!

There is a Tone, a clear sound of wealth that must be broadcast to the universe from your inner self, void of need. If you release a sound of poverty, fear and unbelief then you will receive more of what you already have! All who have the same note, tone, assignment will be magnetized to you, your business. Clients, wealth and health will astound the doubters! Your mind is your personal broadcasting station, thought waves of prosperity, abundance, riches or thought waves of lack, fear and doubt all attract like atoms when released from your being. Increase the frequency of meditation by sending out deliberate thoughts waves of what you desire to create. This will speed up the manifestation process. Your mind will only manifest thru meditation, the place where your spirit becomes one with the divine.

They were all in one accord! One sound, one tone. You must have the same sound in the house, in relationships, in churches to produce the highest yield!

Presidents of Corporations, Vice-presidents, Couples, everybody in your business, leaders in church organizations and multi-level marketing companies must vibrate at the same level to produce the highest level of increase!

Most inner cities produce crime because there is the sound of poverty, sound of anger and notes of unhappiness in side of the people. Remember, rich people live in museums, poor people in jungles, choose your destiny!

Their must be a divine shift in consciousness, understanding that the level of manifestation you are in is only limited by your belief system, psycho self induced fears, and misnomers of your upbringing mindset about your own worth and value. You will limit the possibility of a wealth demonstration.

The universe is user friendly but you have to be in the right state to receive! Chaos, low finances, relationships issues, degree of manifested wealth are all states, subjected to change from within! Remember the Magic, the Genius within has to be released . . . abracadabra.

Business is only an activity of mind in action, resulting from the meditation level of bringing the invisible to the visible realm. Supply is within; resources are a creation of mind over matter.

As you develop the millionaire status mindset, your reality will reflect your own mentality. Jesus never blamed his miss-creations on a devil, and he said the "Father and I are one!" You have to get your mind in a place where you radiate and vibrate at the level of what you desire.

Manifesting at the Highest Level

Millionaires in the Making Training Sessions are available at the eighth grade level, to insert mentally the ideal of wealth and train young minds how to manifest, how to attract the right relationships and the wisdom of investing finances verses accumulating debt. In addition, the training will show you how to become a millionaire by age 30 and avoid pitfalls that most teens make in regards to relationships, late planning and finances.

My relationship with you is based on you're ability to help me fulfill my God assignment! Many cannot fulfill Kingdom assignments because they have unresolved issues and divided vision purpose! God sometimes has to stop something in order to start purpose!

Most individual MANIFESTATIONS is limited to a consciousness that continues to place their blessings in a "someday yonder mode," instead of coming into the IAMNESS of God; I am blessed now, I am wealth now, I am health now, I am a tangible millionaire now. The Nowness of God in mind, the blessings are yea and AMEN IN ELOIM! BECOME WHAT YOU DESIRE!

Never seek anointing; seek responsibility and where you can be more effective, your negative mind wants to keep you with a storefront mentality when you could have international affluence.

Symbols of Royalty:

There are symbols of the kingdom, royal ornaments, crowns, scepters, trumpets, swords, orbs, rings, ranks and authority. Basic understanding of heraldry and knighthood will give a clear revelation of how we conduct ourselves in the kingdom.

The King legislates policy, establish governmental procedures and design the protocol to the government. Most of what's been going on Sunday morning has had nothing to do with kingdom; it's been an exercise of futility. Kingdom has been reduced to a place where spiritual addicts come to get a fix to survive the week ahead.

People who have soul addictions get upset if they don't hear there favorite singer or preacher. Choirs have songs, songs that have no reference of kingdom. People sit through a whole service because there is no glory in the pulpit to cause them to stand in the glory of God.

When the kingdom comes it tears down all our rituals, all our ceremonies and traditional ignorance, there is a divine order to follow. It's time for the Esther church to arise! A great way to get the church to see kingdom is to take a field trip to your state capital and see the kings of the earth make laws. Testimonies are only given to celebrate the victory and decree of the king. A King shall decree a thing and it shall be establish, it manifests itself!

You can only move in the revelation knowledge, which you have received. Hosea 4:5 my people are destroyed due to a lack of knowledge Please don't try to institute all the revelation you received in this book overnight, take the people in layers of growth.

Millionaire Solomon

Solomon's GLORY was unlike any other King in the earth realm. Kings from other countries sat down at his feet to receive substance, to hear AND SEE THE manifestations of his consciousness. He was a master strategist who manifested wealth at ridiculous and crazy levels. You have to place yourself in the right spirit position, attitude, mindset, relationship and environment with rich images, vibrations, team synergy, partnerships that will produce the highest yield. Destiny means connections and reveals where you need to make a disconnection, from religion, from envious friends, culture norms, nonproductive relationships, and wrong vibes and surround thyself with the elegance of a King!

Solomon was more than a Billionaire. Solomon's temple was one of the seven wonders of the then known world. The scripture tells us how the kings and queens of all nations came to hear of the wisdom of Solomon and see the house he had built to the lord, as well as the glory of his kingdom.

One of the accounts in kings and in the chronicles concerned the visit of the gentile queen, the Queen of Sheba. Are you ready to receive an earthly King into your court? We should be positioning ourselves so we can have a visitation of an earthly queen. It tells of how Queen Sheba came from the ends of the earth to hear the Wisdom of Solomon and to behold of his glory.

The Queen of Sheba didn't come to a storefront; she came to a royal palace. **The church should be a preparation place to raise up Kings and Queens to impact Nations**. The Queen of Sheba was overcome with all she heard, saw, and felt, she left with his royal bounty and the richness of his kingdom and royalty left her breathless.

11 Chronicles 9, "And when the Queen of Sheba heard of the fame Solomon, she came to prove him with hard questions at Jerusalem with a very great company, and camels that bear spices, and gold in abundances, and precious stones. When she was come to Solomon, she communed with him all that was in her heart."

"She seen the Wisdom of Solomon, the house he had built, and the meat of his table, the sitting of his servants, the attendance of his ministers, and there apparel. His cupbearer also, and their apparel: and his ascent by which he went up to the house of the lord, and there was no more breath in her."

And she said to the king, "it is a true report which I heard in mine own land of thine acts and thy wisdom, howbeit I believe their words, until I came in mine eyes had seen it, and behold the one half of greatness of thy wisdom was not told me, for thou exceeds the fame that I heard. Happy are thy men, and happy are thy servants, which stand continually before thee."

"And she gave the King and hundred and twenty talents of gold, and of spices great abundances, and precious stones, neither was there such spices as the Queen of Sheba gave King Solomon."

"Moreover the King made a great throne of ivory, and overlaid it with gold. And there were six steps to the throne, with a footstool of gold, which were fasten to the throne and stays on each side of the sitting place and two lions standing on both sides. And twelve lions stood there on the one side and on the other steps, all the drinking vessels of the King were of gold. King Solomon exceeded all the kings of the earth for riches and for wisdom." This is a true picture of kingdom!

"Then Solomon sat on the throne of the lord as King instead of David his father and prospered, and all Israel obeyed him. And all the princes and mighty men sons of David submitted unto him, and bestowed upon him such royalty majesty as had not been seen on any King before."

2 Chronicles 1:1 "and Solomon the son of David was strengthen in his kingdom, and the lord his God was with him, and magnified him exceedingly, Solomon secret to success was that in the night God appeared unto him and said, ask what I shall give unto you, and Solomon said unto God, thou hast showed mercy unto David my father, and hast made me to reign in his stead. Now O, Lord let they promise unto David my father be established: this is an important kingdom principle to raise up covenant sons and daughters in the house of God to faithfully carry the paton and faithfully minister as a priest in the house of God, not to move out of timing tempting to establish works due to anxiety of not waiting before the lord."

Many ministries are born out of impatience; many sons have aborted their inheritance not waiting until their season. Solomon waited on his legacy. Wait on your season change, and if you are a type of Solomon, where is your David? Stay in and submitted to an anointed man of God, some riches are by inheritance in a rich family.

Solomon was made a King by inheritance. Solomon knew his gifts and never did what his brother Absalom did, moved beyond his measure of rule, usurped authority over his father, and end up getting hung in a tree. Watch the spirit of Absalom! God has ordained you to walk in wealth, serve your set man faithfully, without a sense of anxiety.

Many members are always in a hurry, last coming in the temple and the first leaving, good preachers but not faithful to the temple yet desired to rule in the house. Be faithful. Understand whose season it is to celebrate, wait for your season, you will cause an odor to the house or God. Those who wait by course have sweet smell upon them.

Millionaire Summary

You will manifest at the level of vibration of wealth energy around you and inside of you. Your environment, music, words, images, all determine the level of wealth that will be released.

A Prince Inherits All The Riches Of The King!

A. T. Stewart 1803-1876

With a five thousand dollar inheritance, this Scotch-Irish immigrant set up a small dry goods shop in New York in 1823. He out grew that, and built an even more spectacular eight-story-tall "iron palace," which became the world's largest retail store when it opened in 1862. His stores were among the first to offer fixed prices, and they attracted the wealthy and fashionable. The bulk of his fortune, however, was gained through wholesaling and especially through heavy investments in New York City real estate. Dying without an heir, he left his fifty-million-dollar fortune to his wife, who passed control of it to his former attorney, who grossly mismanaged it. Two years later his coffin was stolen from the grave and successfully held for ransom.

Marshall Field 1834-1906

Having started out as an errand boy at a dry foods store in Pittsfield, Massachusetts, by 1865 he was partner in an established Chicago dry goods house. By 1881 he had bought out his two partners and renamed the business Marshal Field and company, and by 1895, despite several severe setbacks, the store was grossing forty million dollars a year. He made up the slogan "the customer is always right," and he introduced openly displayed prices, liberal credit, and the ability to return merchandise (and was first to put a restaurant in a store); he also knew how to both anticipate and create consumer demand.

Andrew Carnegie 1835-1919

In 1848 the twelve-year-old Carnegie immigrated with his impoverished Scottish family to the United States. He began working for the Pennsylvania railroad as a telegrapher and rose to be its superintendent of military transportation during the civil war; he resigned in 1865 to pursue his own opportunities. After 1873 he concentrated on steel and built an empire that controlled every aspect of its manufacture, by the turn of the century, his mills produced more steel than all of Great Britain. In 1901 he sold it all to the newly formed United States steel corporation, retired completely, and became a mega-philanthropist, dissolving almost all his fortune to build public libraries and establish a number of foundations and educational and research institutions.

John Jacob Astor 1763- 1848

He started out in the fur business as a clerk but quickly moved on to work for himself. Exchanging American furs for European firearms and musical instruments, by the 1820's he had built up the largest fur-trading business in the United States.

When the government asked its wealthiest citizens to help fund the war of 18 12, he did his part-clearly to his advantage, paying only eighty-eight cents on the dollar for two million dollars' worth of government bonds. When the fur business began to wane, he coolly sold out and refocused on his already flourishing real estate investments, buying up lots in the desolate northern part of Manhattan and gambling that the growing city would catch up. It did.

William Weightman 1813-1904

He emigrated from England at sixteen at the urging of an uncle who owned a chemical-manufacturing company in Philadelphia and became its chemist, after the deaths of his uncle and his partner, he took over the business. The predecessor of the pharmaceutical company, it was the first to develop and manufacture cheap and effective substitutes for quinine to treat malaria, and it also pioneered the manufacture of citric acid, both a food flavoring and an ingredient in metal polish. He invested conservatively, primarily in land, and became the largest real estate owner in Philadelphia. He was intensely private and shunned society in favor of spending time at home, tending his garden of rare flowers.

Moses Taylor 1806-1882

Growing up surrounded by wealth-his father was John Jacob Astor's confidential agent-he was determined to earn his own. In 1832 he used $15,000 he had saved to open his own import business, which he left in 1 855 to become the president of city bank. During the panic of 1857 he bought controlling interest, for $5 dollars a share, in the ailing Delaware, Lackawanna & Western Railroad, he appeared to have been swept away by his passion for railroads, but seven years later it was trading at $240 a share. His contemporaries regarded his intimate knowledge of his investments as his greatest asset, but he built his lasting reputation on his sense of civic duty: he organized and chaired the committee of bankers that kept the union solvent during the civil war.

Cyrus Curtis 1850- 1933

He left school at sixteen after his family's house burned down and eventually made his way into the newspaper business. In 1879 he started the Tribune and Farmer, which included a column for women written by his wife, the column was so successful that he spun it into Ladies' Home Journal, whose circulation rose to two hundred thousand in its first year and a half. He bought the Saturday Evening Post in 1897 for a thousand dollars and had raised its circulation from two thousand to 2.7 million by the time of his death. He was complimented as a genius for marketing to the average American with a willingness to pay the highest prices for stories by writers like Mark Twain and Louisa May Alcott.

John I. Blair 1802-1899

As a ten-year-old farm boy in New Jersey he supposedly told his mother, "I have seven brothers and three sisters. That's enough in the family to be educated. I am going to get rich." He dropped out of school at eleven to work as a clerk and within seven years had opened his own store. He began in mining, forming the Lackawanna Coal & Iron Company, but made his fortune in railroads. With a little help from political connections, he and some colleagues chartered the union pacific, which built the eastern half of the transcontinental railroad and became infamous for its owners' business practices. At one time he served as president of sixteen railroads simultaneously, had enough acreage to cover half of New Jersey, and personally owned more track then anyone else in the world.

To manifest at the highest level, activate the millionaire law of release.

I now let go of worn out things, worn out conditions, worn out situations, worn out relationships, mindsets, belief systems and addictive worn out habits. I now move forward into happy new experiences where i belong… all ordained in my life now come, all not ordained now make a swift exit!!

Divine intelligence now lock in the right soulmate, the right clients, and the right career for my life. I let go of my nets which have entangled me from expanding and prospering…those who are sent in my life to bless me i receive, those anointed to curse me, I let go.

I deserve to be celebrated, elevated and appreciated!!

I let go of any one, any thing that is no longer apart of the divine plan of my life. I let them swiftly go, they let me go. Life now forgives me of my past mistakes and i now make a fresh covenant with God to experience my jabez!

I now attract the perfect people, rich opportunities, prosperity energy, wealth, and health into my life.

Millionaire Mindset

Manifesting Millionaire Mindset Through Daily Wealth Meditations

Powershift Keys

In order to gain the maximum effectiveness from this **Millionaire Status Book**, you will need to form a new habit within the next 30 days of meditating on these Wisdom principals which will guarantee wealth, health, and prosperity in all realms of your life. Kings live by principles. Confess out boldly these declarations of faith, within 30 days you will see manifestations of riches, wealth around you, **As A Man Thinketh In His Heart So Is He**!

Now get ready to get in what I call the **Solomon Position**. A position of power, intimacy, and prayer with the father of the universe.

Now decree thy kingdom come and experience a complete new world. Practice these principles and manifest riches, love and influence yourself. It's time to shift from religion to Kingdom. You cannot have a thing until you become conscious of it. Seek ye first the king's domain, now let down your nets daily and enclose great abundances of prosperity. It's past time you became an eagle. Eagles live in the air, eagles have great vision, and eagles soar high. Study daily and experience gold as dust!!

Albert Einstein

All existences begin in the Imagination of man, then his will to his reality!

Man's highest ambition shouldn't be centered on self; it should be centered on giving his best, highest gift and contribution to family and community unselfish service to humanity.

Dr. Israel P. Barsh

You Are A Masterpiece In The Making

Business Your World is an activity of spirit and since that spirit is your spirit, business, your world is an activity of your spirit.

Therefore, your business, your world even ***you're universe*** will reflect the conditions of your consciousness. ***Think, feel, see, visualize, see yourself being, doing, having all*....*Taste Success***.

You must ***consciously*** realize each day that business is an activity of God operating through the instrument of one mind, your business success, ***unlimited supply of wealth money is only limited to your shifting of your consciousness to a higher vibration to attract the substance for your unlimited lifestyle***. Vibrate, radiate, dress like that millionaire...***Love Thy Self***.

Business is not subject to weather, people, places, it is subject to your consciousness, you must develop a consciousness of a millionaire.... ***as you meditate so shall you manifest your idea world...so be it....it is....it is finish....I am it now***.

Law Of Restoration

I call on the great Law of Restoration, my good of past and present is now divinely restored, I claim my present blessings, and I am receiving my highest good of mind, body and financial affairs now. The universe now deposits large sums of cash in my account. My money angel now bringeth forth new money, new creative ideals spring forth in my consciousness, I am a creator, I create new things. I am one with the Father economy, one with the Son and one with the Holy Ghost. I ***Am That I Am...***

My Money Decree

I Praise and I Acknowledge the God has my source of supply, within and I make contact with my thoughts. I practice the law of love in all relationships which opens up the door of riches give thanks that the gateway to infinite endless surplus riches, new money, travel and financial freedom now opens wide for me. My business now exceeds sales of ______weekly. God's riches flow freely to more money and me is **circulating in my life**. To the amount I let **circulate**_out is the amount which is multiplied circulating back in my life. I activate the **Law Of Circulation** since money is currency it is designed to **flow**, as it flows out, so it **flows in**. Every day and everywhere I now live by the divine principals which govern the universe. I am a symbol of wealth; money is attracted to me from all points of the universe. I tithe beyond 10 percent which is a law of tithing; I give freely to charity organizations. My money angel now delivers clients unto me at an accelerated level...

The Power Of The Subconscious

Your subconscious is the mind of Eloim. It offers you the creative powers to be wealthy, rich, and healthy. The keys to your very own destiny begin regularly to see your dream into reality, see victory, achievement, new money, estate become a symbol of wealth. Thinking makes it so, place right images daily, at night, and reap millions. Taste it, feel it, become it...***Welcome Holy Spirit . . . Let There Be Light.***

Angelic Assignment

You are here by divine ordination, not by accident, neither coincident, you were predestined at connection by infinite wisdom. You were genetically designed by God, to accomplish great things in life. You are God's original design, express your **greatness**...**Your script was written from eternity to reality**!

I am now surrounded by an innumerable number of angels who have been assigned to me since birth to bring me into the highest purpose of my being in the earth, I am a rich living child of the God of the universe, I am **blessed... wow** I am a positive spirit. ***Thank You Lord Jesus Christ***...Unspeakable joy fills my soul. I am born to win...I am a child of God...Lead me now into my very own royal road of riches...

Now riches appear and are permanent in my life, my bank account is always full of wealth, money and prosperity.

Thoughts Become Our Reality! $$$

Imagination Rules The World. $$$$$

**Imagine Yourself Being It, Doing It,
Having Every One Of Your Desires…$$$$$$$**

I Will Give You The Desires Of Your Heart…$$$$$

Dream It! Visionalize It! $$$$

Believe It Is Done! $$$$$$

Feel It As Reality! $$$$$$$

Taste Success! $$$$$$

Creator's Genes

Genetically you were designed with the DNA of the Maker; you were created with **"Genius Genes".** You were genetic created as God; originally ideal when the Creator created you. Eloim thought of himself, you were created to fulfill his millions of unfulfilled dreams. Tap into your hidden resources… Let divine wisdom guide you, let divine intelligence inspire you, let supreme wisdom of the universe ignite your destiny…You have an innumerable company of angels to bring you into your highest destiny.

State of Desire

All things begin as a thought; **all** things are possible through consciousness, get into the state of desire.

Become one with the father, become one with your neighbors dream. What you make happens for others, God makes happen for you! Give the gift of **love** daily, **love**.

Angel of unconditional **love** cometh! I **am love.**

Let there be…..

Every visible manifestation in your life is a direct result of your expanded individual or collective expanded consciousness.

Infinite intelligence now releases supreme wisdom light and reveals my hidden talents, gifts and skills which I were endowed with by the almighty. Now these gifts open up new doors of unlimited wealth, travel, riches, joy and money overflows my accounts. I am **getting in the Solomon position by applying kindgom principles**.

This knowledge is immediately revealed to my consciousness. I will follow its lead. I live by the laws that govern the universe.

1. Law of cause/effect
2. Law of love
3. Law of tithing
4. Law of prosperity
5. Law of circulation

I am……

I am….. The most powerful decree in the universe is "I am"

When you speak I **am**, everything connected to that name is attracted to you…**I am** is God's first name, what you add to I **am** follows you…**I am** rich,

I **am** blessed, I **am** a millionaire, I **am** wealthy, I **am that I am, I am** health, I **am** peace, I **am** joy, I **am that I am, I am,** life, I **am** fulfilled. I **am** the essence of love, I am a money magnet, I **am** a people magnet, I **am** likeable, I **am that I am**......watch what you add to I **am. Tell** your mind what to think, **tell** your mouth what to speak and **tell** your body how to feel.

I Am That I Am

I am rich, radiant substance of the universe, I **am! I am!** My financial affairs are now filled with this rich radiant universal substance, divine substance cannot be held from me. Divine substance cannot be taken from me. Divine substance is the one and only reality in my financial affairs. Divine substance manifests wealth in all realms of my life. Divine substance is the foundation of all wealth. I **am** all the substance there is. I **am** divine substance. I **am** surrounded by divine substance and it manifests a large financial income for me. Now, I invite the powerful loving substance of the universe to produce abundant supply here and now. My business is surrounded by divine substance and manifest surplus abundant supply for all of my business. **Increase, increase, increase**. Divine substances now manifests new rich clothes, shoes, suits, cars, housing estate, health, wealth, affluence and influence. I **am** so rich with divine substance. My money into my life, my organization now grows over 1000, my business, books, now brings in a secured monthly income over $10,000.00, more freedom to travel, more freedom to have fun, more freedom with my choice relationships. Only good can come out of all situations. I create new realities. I don't depend on people, conditions, weather for my prosperity. I depend on consciousness. I **am that I am**. God is **my** source. My prosperity is permanent. I have become a radiant magnetic symbol of wealth. I generate wealth; create wealth, design wealth on my many different planes. I have a wealth mentality. I visualize money. I **Am Money!!! Money Cometh**.

Psalms 23 Wealth Decree...

The Lord is my banker I shall not lack, infinite wisdom maketh me to lie down in gold mines, yea though I walk thru the valley of debt , I shall fear no bankruptcy or repossession, since I practice tithing I fear no evil , therefore silver and gold flows freely around me, I am become a magnetic symbol of wealth. Surely riches and wealth shall follow me all the days of my life, because I operate in kingdom principals.

Affirmations for Wisdom

1. I awake daily with the thoughts of Jehovah, therefore I practice reading 6 chapters daily of proverbs for wisdom.

2. I practice daily getting rid of any negative feeling, ideal that will hinder my divine self of expression into wealth, health and prosperity.
3. I choose to go to the next level of glory therefore I expect others to not understand my new self, I am that I am, my purpose has CHANGED.
4. In order for me to go up the ladder of success I let some people go.
5. I associate with the rich.
6. Thoughts of my past I can't give a luxury to think in my present.
7. I create wealthy relationships.
8. I produce wealth within.
9. I become a symbol of wealth.
10. I am a money magnet.
11. I am God's choice for this generation
12. If not me then who, if not now then when, if not here then where?

Today I release everything, every thought and everyone who is no longer apart of the divine plan of God for my destiny, I freely release the old people, old habits, old ways, I welcome the new.

Taking the Land Mediation.

I now claim my divine inheritance which is in the saints, riches, wealth, prosperity is my birth right, nothing can withhold my greater good, I now claim the rich blessing of my new car, new house, new relationships, new creative money making ideals which will release permanent success.

I now call forth the angels assigned to me since birth to bring into my life right purpose, right relationships, and divine harmony reign supreme.

My family good is at hand and quickly appear, Millions Now Fills My Bank Account With Ease.

I call on the great law of restoration, the good of the past and present is divinely restored and is permanent in my life. I give thanks for the perfect divine results.

Divine love governs all my affairs, anger, lust; pride has no place in me.

Thy Kingdom Come.

Generational curses in my family, in my past do not come in my future, I let go, God has forgiven me, I forgive myself, I love myself freely.

Kingdom decrees

1. I represent Kingdom in my dress, in my thoughts, I am a rich loving child of the rich loving universe, therefore only good can come in all situations.
2. Kingdom is not church.
3. God is now increasing my worth, my self esteem soars, I am skillfully designed in the image of the Maker, and I am a masterpiece in the making.
4. My money angel now bring new wealth creating ideals, manifested wealth in my life, I am so blessed.
5. Divine intelligence now guides me into the riches, highest purpose; wisdom now governs all my affairs, divine substance is the 1 and only reality in my world.
6. My family is the epitome of excellence, my children walk in wisdom, my sons and daughters steps are ordered by God.
7. I give above 10%.
8. I am now surrounded by an innumerable company of angels who brings peace, prosperity in all realms of life.
9. At the opening of my lips wisdom is released, in the company of people they are amazed at the Wisdom of Solomon which illuminate there world.
10. Money is currency, therefore I let it flow.
11. My mind is the incubator of God; I exercise every thought, ideal, habit out of my life.
12. I get in the flow of wealth.
13. I am genetically designed as a God.
14. I live like the rich and famous.
15. My latter end shall be greater than my former.
16. I am a channel of international influence.
17. I daily make contact with the divine source within me, God inside of me consciousness.
18. Infinite wisdom now governs all my decisions, now the gateway of right relationships, right careers, and now manifests large abundances blessings of permanent prosperity.

19. Divine spirit is my supply, infinite intelligence knows my future, my gifts, my talents, and my worth, my value now increases, infinite wisdom now releases me from the past to a brand new future. New doors of expression.

Angelic Assignment

You are here by divine ordination, not by accident, neither coincident, you were predestined at connection, you were predestined at birth, you were not born into a curse, you were created as a masterpiece in the making.

The Manifestation Process

Jesus said I am the way, the truth, the life, he didn't ask you to study truth, he asked you to become truth.

You will become what you think about; you are an outward manifestation of your inward heart. You were genetically design by God to accomplish great things in life.

1. To know a man watch his daily habits
2. To walk in kingdom riches you must practice kingdom principals.

What your eyes see, you will become, watch what you place your eyes upon, and some people in your life were not God ordained, you just kept looking at them.

Power Of The Subconscious

Your subconscious is the mind of the maker, your conscious is the programmer, and subconscious is the producer. By you placing right thoughts in memory bank, right actions will produce over time.

1. All things begin as thoughts.
2. Business is an activity of your spirit, since that spirit is your spirit; you become the buyer and seller in mind.
3. Therefore your business world and universe will reflect your consciousness.
4. Business is not subject to weather, people, places, it is subject to your thoughts, think right thoughts, stop blaming people of your conditions.
5. Many of you have on the radio, but you are on the wrong channel.
6. Wealth is a symbol.
7. Place right symbol in mind and reap right results.
8. I and the father are one; I am one with the father economy.

Millionaire Mindset

A Millionaire Mindset. What level of mindset do you have, your reality reflects your present mentality. God has no problem with the amount of zero's on your check, whether it's 5 or 6 digit monthly income is solely up to you, according to your faith be it unto you, it's amazing how Christian people can believe God for healing, deliverances, cast out demons, but yet to cast out debt, cast out bad credit, cast out low finances in their churches. You will never acquire wealth with a religious mindset, money chases creative ideas. If God can get you out of sin, then that same God if you practice kingdom principles will get you debt free! Locate where you are, then locate what level of prosperity, tangible income you desire to enjoy. Have a game plan to accomplish the dream goal.

When you see other's living in fancy million dollar estates, riding in the newest BMW, eating at the finest restaurants, dining in elegance, wearing the clothe line of the latest , hottest fashions from Paris, how do you react? Do you bless them, or do you say, who does she think she is? Well if you curse the rich, the rich you will never be, if you bless the rich then you will become the rich, wealth, affluence, influence, money escapes the minds and the hands of the unkind, and unskilled.

Millionaires are born in all walks of life, matriculates from all sizes of the community, a famous Amos, a Walt Disney, a Howard Hughes. Is there a certain personality, certain genetic trait, is there simply an innate hungry for life? Certain ingredients are essential; you can't place a large dream in a small minded person. A new consciousness, new mindset, agreeable relationships, must be developed are few of the many characteristics of tangible multimillionaires in society. When you study modem day successful and highly famous individuals, despite their past, become Champions in a variety of arena's such as, Leonardo da Vinci, Henry Ford, Albert Einstein, Nelson Mandela, there are no two fingerprints. The Steve Wonder's, Steven Spielberg's, Oprah Winfrey's of life, the Elvis Presley's, Bill Gate's, the Maya Angelo's, the Fred Price's, Martin Luther King's all resolved they have a higher purpose to serve the earth, and refined themselves to serve the greater purpose. The attribute to bounce back in life, find the angel within you becomes the Holy Grail, the golden key to the next level. Find your Gethsemane and stay there until as Job said until my change comes.

Millionaire status therefore is not just about the Benjamin's, the tangibles of life, it's about the Fighter within a man, the desire to release your gift to the world, in spite of difficult, knowing that out of the tomb of hopelessness came the master of the universe, when the odds are against you, then this is your greatest moments. True riches within your grasp cannot always be measured in money, put this philosophy of millionaire status in consciousness, Have a resolve today, don't allow problems to paralyze you, to sabotage your destiny, or destroy relationships, allow your setbacks to become set up's for future Miracles. Take a break in life, but swing back, Smile big, laugh, pray long, give generously, forgive quickly, love deeply, hold a child often, and live on the sunny side of the mountain.

Certain attributes which were in George Washington Carver are in all, which would depict many as geniuses, in reality they found something they loved to do and they sacrificed, they were RISK Takers. Think of a Frank Wright, greatest architect in history, Pablo Picasso, greatest artist of the twentieth century, a Michael Jordan, greatest basketball player of the 2 1 century. These people defied the odds, refused to quit, and refused to bow to others when told it couldn't be done. They thirst, hunger for the better life!

When faced by a mountain, I will not quit, I will continue to climb, or I will stay there, make a tunnel through it, or simply sit on it and turn it to a gold mine!

Millionaire Key: In order to attract wealth into your life, your subconscious mind must be open to the ideal of wealth flowing toward you.

You have to trick your mind, and your subconsciousness is the server of the master key which is your consciousness. If you can dream it, you can achieve it, but dream big, the universe cannot fill small orders! Ask for the moon, even if you land on a star!

Einstein said, Imagination is Creation. Consciousness creates everything! Proverbs stated as a man thinketh in his heart so is he. Become consciousness of what you want. Develop a Millionaire consciousness, or a Billionaire consciousness, you cannot attract wealth with a good-will, poverty consciousness, religious some day soon mentality. You have to destroy the slave wage mentality. Dress your mind up to where you are going not where you been! Play music in your environment fit for Kings, get in the right vibrations, symphony, Beethoven, and create the mood for creativity. Sometime the wrong tone can produce a negative experience.

Locate thyself, what's holding you back from getting that college degree, starting you own business, writing your first book, traveling to exotic island with your love one, who is pulling your heart string away from God's ordained plan for your life, if it's baking cakes, if it's cooking chicken, if it's making the best clothes, if it's singing, then refine thyself, define thyself, don't allow other people opinions of you define you, remember Colonel Sander's knock on 999 doors until he finally received one yes, and today, Kentucky Fried Chicken Franchise's are on each block in America and International.

Your optimist attitude must break forth from the pessimist crowd who will smother and kill your dream.

Get up NOW and soar as the eagles without boundaries, find the thing you love to do, and do it well and then at your doorstep will be riches! One thing I warn you to never do, never give in to defeat, never give up on your dream, never accept failure, don't be a clone to someone else pains, some one else loneliness, you owe it to your self to be happy, fulfilled, and you deserve the best in life, realize losses are upside down crosses which turn into triumphs on tomorrow! Never rehearse your past, bury it in the sands of yesterday, and dig new wells of prosperity today!

Millionaire in Greek means, abundantly supplied, without having lack, the ability to become self reliance is the heart of every living being in the earth, all came to earth with a million dollar idea inside of them, with a God changing idea locked between the corridors of their consciousness.

There are white millionaires, Hispanic millionaires, African millionaires, millionaires of all races, and the astronomical power of purpose lives within a man, not outside of him/her. God never went outside himself for anything, the creative ability of the creator of the universe placed in you power to manifest wealth. You will see that self made millionaires are made daily, one thing that all have in common and most millionaires agree that there are opportunities everywhere, what other call junk, become other's wealth producing ideals.

Rich people, poor people have a different mindset, have different energy, they radiate, they vibrate at a different level, they think, they react, they dream different! Many can see the angel in the rock, many can see the diamonds in coals, many can hear the masterpiece in the song, and others don't even listen. You have to learn how to turn a silver moment into a golden opportunity. It's never too late to start, if you start now, instead of waiting for your laid off slip, go in and fire yourself to the NEXT LEVEL OF LIVING, where you are the author, conductor, and the finisher of your destiny. Grasp the mindset of a millionaire, let go of your yesterday tears and move into your millionaire status years.

W. Clement with only $100.00 the desire to succeed and employing the principles in Think and Grow Rich was able to build an organization that now produces a gross annual income of over thirty-six million Dollars.

Madame C.J. Walker in 1867-1918

Madame C. J. Walker grew up in poverty, unable to read or write, surviving one hardship after another. She was born in 1867 in Louisiana; she went from being a wash woman to being the first woman millionaire through experimenting with various mineral and animal oils to find a remedy for her hair falling out. Constructed a Plant in Pittsburgh, where she founded the Leila College of Beauty, start the Walker Enterprise, provided employment for some 3000 employees in 1905.

Arthur G. Gaston in 1892-1996

Grew up in Demopolis, Alabama, born July 4, 1892, Gaston personal dream was to empower African Americans socially and economically, he and his wife pioneered the Booker T. Washington Business college. Gaston during the heat of the Civil rights movement started the Citizens Federal Saving Bank Association; by 196 1 its assets exceeded $5 million. Founded the A. G. Boys Club, his bank became the largest in Alabama.

John H. Johnson 1918-2006

First African American to succeed a major magazine publishing Ebony and Jet magazines, the world's largest African American -owed publishing company. The company has more than 3000 thousand employees and sales annually over $350 million. Johnson used his mother furniture as a security for a $500.00 loan, sent out 20,000 copies of a letter offering charter subscriptions to his new magazine, 3000 people send in $2 annual giving him $6000.00 to start his dream!

Quincy D. Jones born 1933 One of the highly acclaimed celebrated artists in the world, Quincy Jones began playing music at an early age, active in high school band and music, wrote first composition in high school "From the four Winds". Moved to Seattle Washington, toured the clubs experience the music of great musicians such as Dizzy Gillespie, Charlie Parker, Duke Ellington. Won scholarships to study music at the University of Washington, Schillinger's house, and Boston Institution. Producer of recording by Michael Jackson, Tevin Campbell, Keith Washington, the Winans and many more.

The Divine has only one entry in the earth, thru the birth canal of all substance, man's unlimited imagination, unleashing millions of dreams from eternity to reality (Philippians 3:13, l 4) now the past stretches forward to your future.

Children's decree

I decree over my children they all walk in divine revelation wisdom insight, they are full of the holy spirit, angels surround them daily, loading them with skillful wisdom, insights, inventions, they are in covenant with Jehovah, integrity and truth is at the entry of their heart, daily I teach them to practice there faith, they turn many teenagers to the kingdom of light, prosperity is their portion, they dream big dreams.

Wisdom of kings and queens is released at the opening of their lips, their minds are lighting quick to absorb, remember facts, events, equations, algebra, calculus, physics, economics and understand the times, many are in the field of property ownership, money manifests all around them, they are mangers of business, they excel beyond their peers in knowledge, science, academics and athletics, they are full of pure light energy producing the mindset of millionaires, our children walk in, decree wealth, health, protection, riches circulate in their world, they understand true submission of fathers and honoring mothers, our sons and daughters excel in the Nation, only good comes their way.

Each day I create the right energy to receive the right result, I practice walking in love toward all, I bless all around me! I release anything, any one that attaches negative energy unto me; I stay non attached to those who seek to undermine my divine purpose.

As a single believer I walk in divine agreement covenant with God, I set myself in the position to operate in wisdom in relationship, virtue, holiness, I exercise dominion over any desires that outside of the plan of God for my life, I link with my higher purpose, I ask the holy spirit to guide me to my higher self, I create the right energy to produce the right results in my finances, I place the symbol of money, wealth in my consciousness, I practice tithing to my church, I practice giving offerings , my good comes easy, in times of distress I mediate , I concentrate on the desired results, I practice reading my mediation prayer daily, I see myself growing, I see myself in divine alignment with purpose, I call on my angels , the lord of host to intervene in all my affairs. I request angelic help daily, at night I move into visions and dreams manifesting wealth, health, prosperity, new money in my life, I see $thousands of dollars deposited in my account, I see my self debt free, it feels so good, I see my self serving my higher purpose for humanity and the world! Divine substance is my only reality.

Daily Covenant Prosperity Decrees 100 Fold Blessings!

I today decide to seize every waking hour for the Kingdom Mandate of dominion to be fulfill in all realms of my life, I call my self blessed, even if the blessing has not yet manifested from the visible to the invisible, I call my self blessed, I now embrace the new season in my life, I take control of my time, I don't waste any time with time wasters, I manage what the universe has given me and it increases, I fret over nothing, I am so blessed! I call my family blessed,

I Now comprehend and understand there is a divine shifting going on in me, God is taking me out of the pits making me a candidate to Rule In Life, my flesh, my disobedience to kingdom principals has cause me to be behind schedule, today I decide to kill the flesh! To allow spirit to rule in all levels of life, I no longer fulfill the desires of my flesh, I now choose complete obedience! I cut a fresh covenant which will cause me, my descendants , my seed to be blessed,

I released every sabotaging thought, attitude, habit, person which has impeded the hand of God, I consecrate my life to the glory of the father.

I invoke and surround myself now with the Angels assigned since birth to manifest the divine path of abundances , prosperity, right divine relationships, my very own royal road to riches, growth to our church, growth in our business, property ownership, debt free, business ownership, travel to foreign countries, to impact nations!

I am a child of destiny, I welcome the person of the Holy spirit to allow wisdom and revelation knowledge to govern all my affairs, govern all my waking decisions where I now become a Money Magnet attracting wealth, riches, prosperity, and a people magnet attracting all the right clients who will network with my business causing us to make our first Million Dollars!

I place the prosperity symbol within, as a man thinketh so is his reality. Money is no longer my boss, it is my servant! To establish Kingdom.

Every cell in my body from the crown of my head to my feet, all my vital organs, my eyes, my mind, my brain, my lungs, heart, liver, nose, throat, pancreas, all upper, lower intestines, all work perfect, I drink my $H2^0$ daily, my kidney, all body parts, ears, respiratory system, sinusitis, feelings, alertness, muscles, all work perfect! When friends see me they see the fountain of youth, I practice giving praise, smile is my style! I let go of all negative images of my past, it is not allowed to come in my present, I exhale the old, and I inhale the new. And it feels so good, no negative word, no negative person is attracted to me, as I am within, I attract without, I am the cause and the effect of my life thru Jesus Christ.

Infinite wisdom supreme intelligence now is released to my mind causing new ideals to attract wealth into my life, I now break the poverty curse from my family, from my life, creating the wholeness I so desire!

I cancel debt out of my life, I make wise money choices, I invest my first 10% to God, the 2nd 10 % to myself, and I tithe by faith and not by sight. My money now makes money! I don't work for money. Money works for me! Divine substance now manifests large finances for me now, I am rich, radiate wealth, my mind is a wealth magnet, divine substance prospers me, I now invites the divine substance to manifest here and now, I always have abundant of supply, my consciousness is my only currency, abundant is everywhere! I no longer strain and strive, I tithe and thrive, and I now come into the 100 fold blessings!

God deposited millions of creative genes inside of me, I am a masterpiece in the making, because I tithe above 10% of all my personal and business earnings, I now experience wealth at the **next level!**

I am the epitome of excellence, I walk in the highest integrity with all in my world, and the angels assigned to me since birth now bring me into the riches, most successful plan, and relationships of my life! And it feels so good, I freely let go of my past, I forgive easily, my past freely let go of me, any thing, anybody who are no loner apart of the divine plan of my life I freely let go, I make room for the divine connections , relationships, new money, new clients to come in!

At the opening of my lips is wisdom, supreme wisdom, kingly revelation is revealed to me as I meditate so my world manifests, as it is within, so it is without.

Amazing Astounding Extraordinary Magnificent Genius

Ability is released to my mind, I am that I am!

In all my affairs I exalt God, only good can come, divine substance is my one and only reality, I am clothed with supernatural expert wisdom which causes me to become an International Icon!

A king surrounds himself with symbols of his kingdom, I practice silence mediation daily, from my consciousness unfolds abundances in my world, I see tremendous turn around in my finances, I create from within, I am a wealth creator, I create new money making ideals, I send love vibrations, I send love thoughts to all around me, I expect therefore I receive,

Because I tithe I am one with the fathers economy, because I tithe I am not afraid of what the world economy is going thru, God is my Source!

I am complete In Christ, I am made whole, well, and my health is great!

I am God intoxicated , not religious indoctrinated, I am a Son of the Most High, the anointing of prosperity is upon my life, I practice holiness in all levels , I now call upon , I summon the Angelic Lord of the host to intervene, super rule in all places in me, govern my steps, my thoughts, my actions produces kingdom! I come into and bring others into the 100 fold blessings.

I Am A Millionaire In The Making Daily Meditation Prayer!

Today I decide right here, right now to declare all around me is blessed! I cut a fresh covenant to manifest as Abraham seed, "I will make you a blessing, your blessings shall overtake you, I will make you the head and not the tail, my latter shall be greater than my former, my word will not return void, I walk under a F.O.G. The Favor Of God!! I invoke my divine Angels to manifest wealth, health, joy and bring me into my very own royal road to riches!!

My Money Angel brings today new wealth tangible substance into my reality, divine substance is my only reality, divine creativity, and intelligence flows unlimited, unhindered thru me. Thru consciousness I attract the right clients who purchase large orders from my business, as it is within so it is without;

I create, manufacture, produce, & design wealth at many different levels. My mind is the mind of the creator of the universe, now large deposits of wealth, new money manifests in my bank account, I invest in more mutual funds, stocks and bonds and it feels so good! I am financially secured!

Business is an activity of spirit, therefore my business income weekly triples, it is not subject to weather, climate, conditions, the buyer & seller are one in mind, I meditate so it manifests, I am that I am, I go within to manifest large incomes, thy kingdom come!! Because I tithe above 105, because I give offerings above 10% there is always 3 things in my house:

1. Divine Overflow of Provisions
2. Fruit of supplies, creativity, physical health, mental strength, spiritual joy & power! Authority over all my adversaries!
3. Twenty-four Hour Angelic Protection

I go within to manifest new cars, new estates, new clients, new associates, new relationships, new energy, radiate health, perfect relationships, new travel, my world is complete and perfect, my business explodes around the world internationally, and my church grows, perfect in consciousness, perfect in reality! I see, I feel, I vibrate, I radiate at the level of a millionaire, and life is so sweet! I go within or I go without...

Kingdom Decree for PROSPERITY....

Thou shalt make thy way prosperous and then shalt thou have good success

Divine intelligence now reveals creative ways, ideals, better ways of conducting, increasing and producing my business

Divine intelligence now releases creative ideals, techniques of creating wealth producing results in all realms of my life

Divine supreme wisdom is now revealed to me as I dream, as I meditate how to increase my productivity in life

Now my health, wealth, joy, finances increases...

My good now multiply exceedingly

I tithe above 10 % and the universe pours wealth creating powers into my mind, I attract the right clients to my business, to my church

My good is now overflowing…

If I can think it up I can think it down

I mental rehearse all my success

Poverty and prosperity is a principle working in me, I choose to allow prosperity to operate in my subconscious

I now move from a comfort level of being an employee to an employer

Thoughts are things

I vibrate, I radiate at over $10,000.00 monthly

Life is addition not subtraction, if anyone in your life is subtracting from you then you need to release them.

Convey to your mind the idea of a million dollar, through concentration, focus, clear thought, clear vision, your subconscious will release it

Manifest kingdom, I now gives thanks for the perfect, harmonious solution which takes place through the wisdom of the Almighty.